Learning Groovy 3

Java-Based Dynamic Scripting

Second Edition

Adam L. Davis

Apress®

Learning Groovy 3: Java-Based Dynamic Scripting

Adam L. Davis
New York, NY, USA

ISBN-13 (pbk): 978-1-4842-5057-0   ISBN-13 (electronic): 978-1-4842-5058-7
https://doi.org/10.1007/978-1-4842-5058-7

Managing Director, Apress Media LLC: Welmoed Spahr
Acquisitions Editor: Steve Anglin
Development Editor: Matthew Moodie
Coordinating Editor: Mark Powers

Cover designed by eStudioCalamar

Cover image designed by Freepik (www.freepik.com)

Distributed to the book trade worldwide by Springer Science+Business Media New York, 233 Spring Street, 6th Floor, New York, NY 10013. Phone 1-800-SPRINGER, fax (201) 348-4505, e-mail orders-ny@springer-sbm.com, or visit www.springeronline.com. Apress Media, LLC is a California LLC and the sole member (owner) is Springer Science + Business Media Finance Inc (SSBM Finance Inc). SSBM Finance Inc is a **Delaware** corporation.

For information on translations, please e-mail editorial@apress.com; for reprint, paperback, or audio rights, please email bookpermissions@springernature.com.

Apress titles may be purchased in bulk for academic, corporate, or promotional use. eBook versions and licenses are also available for most titles. For more information, reference our Print and eBook Bulk Sales web page at http://www.apress.com/bulk-sales.

Any source code or other supplementary material referenced by the author in this book is available to readers on GitHub via the book's product page, located at www.apress.com/9781484250570. For more detailed information, please visit http://www.apress.com/source-code.

Printed on acid-free paper

To my parents, to whom I owe everything in ways large and small.

To my children, who mean the world to me.

To my wife, for putting up with me and supporting me.

Table of Contents

About the Author

 **Adam L. Davis** makes software. He has spent many years developing in Java (since Java 1.2) and has enjoyed using Spring and Hibernate. Since 2006 he's been using Groovy and Grails in addition to Java to create SaaS web applications that help track contracts and finances for large institutions (among other things) at The Solution Design Group, Inc.

Adam has a master's and a bachelor's degree in Computer Science from Georgia Tech. He attends many conferences, has authored several books, and sometimes speaks at conferences and his local Java User Group.

You can find out more at his web site: `www.adamldavis.com`.

He currently resides in Central Florida with his wife, two small children, and their dog.

About the Technical Reviewer

Manuel Jordan Elera is an autodidactic developer and researcher who enjoys learning new technologies for his own experiments and creating new integrations.

Manuel won the 2010 Springy Award—Community Champion and Spring Champion 2013. In his little free time, he reads the Bible and composes music on his guitar. Manuel is known as `dr_pompeii`. He has tech-reviewed numerous books for Apress, including *Pro Spring, Fourth Edition* (2014), *Practical Spring LDAP* (2013), *Pro JPA 2, Second Edition* (2013), and *Pro Spring Security* (2013).

Read his 13 detailed tutorials about many Spring technologies, contact him through his blog at `www.manueljordanelera.blogspot.com`, and follow him on his Twitter account `@dr_pompeii`.

Acknowledgments

Thank you to the following people without whom this book would not have been possible: my wife, for putting up with me working on yet another book; my editors, for all of the much needed editing; and my technical reviewer, Manual Jordan Elera, for doing the vital work of making sure everything in this book is accurate. Thank you to all of the developers behind Groovy and related projects written about in this book: Paul King, Cédric Champeau, Daniel Sun, and the rest of the Groovy team; Peter Niederwieser, the creator of Spock; Luke Daley and the rest of the contributors behind Ratpack; Adam Murdoch, and the rest of the developers behind Gradle; Graeme Rocher and the rest of the team behind Grails and Micronaut; and anyone else I've left out. Without these great tools and frameworks (and the openness, helpfulness, and friendliness of the community), programming would be much less enjoyable.

About This Book

This book is organized into several chapters, starting from the most basic concepts. If you already understand a concept, you can safely move ahead to the next chapter. Although this book concentrates on Groovy, it also refers to other languages, such as Java, Scala, and JavaScript.

As the title suggests, this book is about learning Groovy but will also cover related technology, such as build tools and web frameworks.

Assumptions

This book assumes the reader already is familiar with Java syntax and basic programming ideas.

Icons

Tips   If you see text stylized like this, it is extra information that you might find helpful.

Info   Text stylized this way is usually a reference to additional information for the curious reader.

Warnings   Text like this is caution for the wary reader—many have fallen on the path of computer programming.

Exercises   This is an exercise. We learn by doing. These are highly recommended.

PART I

Getting Groovy

To get started you need to learn the basics of Groovy.

CHAPTER 1

Software to Install

Before you begin programming, you need to install some basic tools.

Java/Groovy

For Java and Groovy, you will need to install the following:

- JDK (Java Development Kit), such as JDK 11

- IDE (Integrated Development Environment), such as IntelliJ IDEA or NetBeans

- Groovy

 Install Java and an IDE

Download and install the Java JDK 11[1] and IntelliJ IDEA.[2]

 **Install Groovy**

Go and install Groovy[3] 3.

---

[1]www.oracle.com/technetwork/java/javase/downloads/index.html
[2]www.jetbrains.com/idea/download/index.html
[3]http://groovy-lang.org/

© Adam L. Davis 2019
A. L. Davis, *Learning Groovy 3*, https://doi.org/10.1007/978-1-4842-5058-7_1

You can download Groovy from `https://groovy-lang.org` and install it. If you install it manually, you may need to set the `JAVA_HOME` environment variable to the location of your Java installation and `GROOVY_HOME` to the location of your groovy installation.

For an easier experience, you may optionally use SDKMAN to install Java and Groovy using "sdk install java" and "sdk install groovy" on the command line. Go to sdkman.io to download it.

Trying It Out

After installing Groovy, you should use it to try coding. Open a command prompt and type `groovyConsole` and press enter to begin.

✎ In the Groovy Console, type the following and then press Ctrl+R to run the code and Ctrl+W to clear the output:

```
1    print "hello"
```

You should keep the Groovy Console open and use it to try all of the examples in this book.

GroovyConsole

File   Edit   View   History   Script   Help

```
1  print "hello"
```

```
groovy> print "hello"

hello
```

Others

Once you have the preceding software installed, you should probably install the following:

- SDKMAN[4]—The Software Development Kit Manager

- Git[5]—A version control program

- Gradle[6]—The build tool

- Grails[7]—The monolithic web framework

Go ahead and install these if you're in the mood—I'll wait.

Code on GitHub

A lot of the code from this book is available at `https://github.com/adamldavis/learning-groovy`.[8] You can go there at any time to follow along with the book.

---

[4]`http://sdkman.io/`
[5]`http://git-scm.com/`
[6]`https://gradle.org/install/`
[7]`https://grails.org/`
[8]`https://github.com/adamldavis/learning-groovy`

CHAPTER 2

Groovy 101

In this chapter, we are going to cover the basics of Groovy, the history of Groovy, and the advantages of using Groovy.

What Is Groovy?

Groovy is a flexible open source language built for the JVM (Java Virtual Machine) with a Java-like syntax. It can be used dynamically (where any variable can hold any type of object) or statically typed (where the type of each variable is heavily restricted); it's your choice. In most other languages, it is one or the other. It supports functional programming constructs, including first-class functions, currying, and more. It has multiple inheritance, type inference, and meta-programming.

Groovy began in 2003 partly as a response to Ruby. Its main features were dynamic typing, meta-programming (the ability to change classes at runtime), and tight integration with Java. Although its original creator left it around 2005, many developers[1] in the community have contributed to it over the years. Various organizations have supported the development of Groovy in the past, and like many open source projects, it cannot be attributed to one person or company. It has been an Apache Software Foundation[2] project since 2015.

---

[1]http://melix.github.io/blog/2015/02/who-is-groovy.html
[2]http://apache.org/

© Adam L. Davis 2019
A. L. Davis, *Learning Groovy 3*, https://doi.org/10.1007/978-1-4842-5058-7_2

Groovy is very similar in syntax to Java, so it is generally easy for Java developers to learn (Java code is generally valid Groovy code, especially since Groovy 3.0, which added support for Java-like array declarations and many other Java syntax features). However, Groovy has many additional features and relaxed syntax rules: closures, dynamic typing, meta-programming (via metaClass), optional semicolons, regex support, operator overloading, GStrings, and more. Groovy is interpreted at runtime, but in Groovy 2.0, the ability to compile to byte-code and enforce type-checking were added to the language.

Compact Syntax

Groovy's syntax can be made far more compact than Java. For example, the following code in Standard Java 5+ should print out "Rod":

```
1    for (String it : new  String[] {"Rod", "Carlos", "Chris"})
2          if (it.length() < 4)
3                System.out.println(it);
```

The same thing can be expressed in Groovy in one line as the following:

```
1    ["Rod", "Carlos", "Chris"].findAll{it.size() < 4}.
     each{println it}
```

It has tons of built-in features to make this possible (compact list definition, extensions to JDK objects, closures, optional semicolons, println method, and optional parentheses).

The method findAll traverses the list and uses the given test to create a new collection with only the objects that pass the test.

Dynamic def

A key feature of Groovy is dynamic typing using the def keyword. This keyword replaces any type definition, thereby allowing variables to be of any type. This is somewhat like defining variables as Object but not exactly the same because the Groovy compiler treats def differently. For example, you can use def and still use the @TypeChecked annotation, which we will cover later.

List and Map Definitions

Groovy makes list and map definitions much more concise and simple. You simply use brackets ([ ]) and the mapping symbol (:) for mapping keys to values:

```
1  def list = [1, 2]
2  def map = [cars: 2, boats: 3]
3  println list.getClass() // java.util.ArrayList
4  println map.getClass() // java.util.LinkedHashMap
```

By default, Groovy interprets map key values as strings without requiring quotes. When working with maps with String keys, Groovy makes life much easier by allowing you to refer to keys using dot-notation (avoiding the get and put methods). For example:

```
1  map.cars = 2
2  map.boats = 3
3  map.planes = 0
4  println map.cars // 2
```

This even makes it possible to Mock objects using a map when testing in some cases (which is covered in a later chapter).

Groovy lists even override the left shift operator (<<), which allows the following syntax example:

```
1  def list = []
2  list.add(new  Vampire("Count Dracula", 1897))
3  // or
4  list << new  Vampire("Count Dracula", 1897)
5  // or
6  list += new  Vampire("Count Dracula", 1897)
```

Tip   Groovy allows overriding of common operators like plus and minus. We will cover this in a later chapter.

Groovy GDK

Built-in Groovy types (the GDK) are much the same as Java's except that Groovy adds tons of methods to every class.

For example, the "each" method allows you to iterate over a collection as follows:

```
1  ["Java", "Groovy", "Scala"].each{ println it }
```

The println and print methods are shorthand for calling those methods on System.out. We will cover the GDK more in depth later.

Everything Is an Object

Unlike in Java, primitives can be used like objects at any time, so there appears to be no distinction. For example, since the GDK adds the `times` method to `Number`, you can do the following:

```
1   100.times { println "hi" }
```

This would print "hi" 100 times.

Easy Properties

Groovy takes the idea of Java Beans to a whole new level. You can get and set Bean properties using dot-notation (and Groovy automatically adds getters and setters to your classes if you don't).

For example, instead of `person.getFirstName()`, you can use `person.firstName`. When setting properties, instead of `person.setFirstName("Bob")` you can just use `person.firstName = 'Bob'`.

🔑 Tip   Unlike Java, Groovy always defaults to public.

You can also easily get a list of all properties of an object in Groovy using `.properties`. For example:

```
1   println person.properties
```

✏️ Tip   Use `properties` to explore some class in Groovy that you want to know more about.

11

GString

Groovy adds its own class, called GString, which allows you to embed Groovy code within strings. This is another feature that makes Groovy very concise and easy to read. A GString is created every time you use double quotes ("") in Groovy.

For example, it makes it easy to embed a bunch of variables into a string:

```
1   def os = 'Linux'
2   def cores = 2
3   println("Cores: $cores, OS: $os, Time: ${new Date()}")
```

The dollar sign $ allows you to refer directly to variables, and ${code} allows you to execute arbitrary Groovy code when included in a Gstring.

Since String is a final class in the JDK, it cannot be extended, so GString is not a subclass of String. Although it can be used in place of String in most places within Groovy code, this can cause some issues when a java.lang.String is needed.

🔑 Tip   If you just want to use a java.lang.String, you should use single quotes ('foo').

Closures

A *closure* is a block of code in Groovy, which may or may not take parameters and return a value. It's similar to lambda expressions in Java 8 or an inner class with one method. Closures can be extremely useful in many ways, which will be covered in subsequent chapters. For example, closures are used by the findAll, each, and times methods, as you have already seen.

Groovy closures have several implicit variables:

- it—If the closure has one argument, it can be referred to implicitly as it.

- this—Refers to the enclosing class.

- owner—The same as this unless it is enclosed in another closure. For example, run the following code to see the difference:

```
def print1 = {list ->
    list.each{println owner}  //prints first Closure
    println owner}         //prints the enclosing class
print1([1,2])
```

- delegate—Usually the same as owner but you can change it (this allows the methods of delegate to be in the scope of the closure).

Closures can be passed as method arguments. When this is done (*and it is the last argument*), the closure may go outside the parentheses. For example, when using the collect method (which uses the given closure to transform elements of list into a new list), you can call it as follows:

```
1  def list = ['foo','bar']
2  def newList = []
3  list.collect( newList ) {
4    it.toUpperCase()
5  }
6  println newList //   ["FOO",    "BAR"]
```

Q Tip   The return keyword is completely optional in Groovy.
A method or closure simply returns its last expression, as seen
previously.

You can also assign closures to variables and call them later:

```
1   def  closr = {x -> x + 1}
2   println( closr(2) ) // prints 3
```

✏ Exercise   Create a closure and print out the class of its
delegate using getClass().

A Better Switch

Groovy's switch statement is much like Java's, except that it allows many
more case expressions. For example, it allows strings, lists, ranges, and
classtypes:

```
1   def x = 42
2   switch ( x ) {
3   case "foo":
4        result = "found foo"
5           break
6    case [4, 5, 6]:
7        result = "4 5 or 6"
8        break
9    case 12..30: // Range
10       result = "12 to 30"
11       break
```

```
12    case Integer:
13         result = "was integer"
14         break
15    case Number:
16         result = "was number"
17         break
18    default:
19         result = "default"
20    }
```

In this case the result from this code will be "was integer".

Meta-Programming

In Groovy, you can add methods to classes at runtime, even to core Java libraries. For example, the following code adds the upper method to the String class:

```
1    String.metaClass.upper = { -> toUpperCase() }
```

or for a single instance (str)

```
1 def str = "test"
2 str.metaClass.upper = { -> toUpperCase() }
```

The upper method would convert the String to uppercase:

```
1    str.upper() == str.toUpperCase()
```

Static Type Checking

If you add the @TypeChecked annotation to your class, it causes the compiler to enforce compile time type-checking. It will infer types for you, so your code can still be *Groovy*. It infers the Lowest Upper Bound (LUB) type based on your code. For example:

```
1  import    groovy.transform.*
2  @TypeChecked
3  class Foo {
4      int i = 42.0 // this does not compile
5  }
1  import    groovy.transform.*
2  @TypeChecked
3  class Foo {
4      int i = 42 // this works fine
5  }
6  new Foo()
```

⚠️ **Gotcha's**   Runtime meta-programming won't always work! In other words, if you add a method using the metaClass and call it, that won't compile.

Explicit type is needed in a closure: a.collect {**String** it -> it.toUpperCase()}

If you add the @CompileStatic annotation to your class or method, it causes the compiler to compile your Groovy code to Java-style byte-code. This would be useful when you have code that needs to be extremely performant (computation involving large lists of Integers, for example) or you need Java byte-code for some other reason. The generated byte-code is almost identical to compiled Java, and therefore the performance is nearly identical to Java (unlike @TypeChecked which still uses Groovy's MOP—Meta Object Protocol). Both annotations are located in the groovy.transform package.

For example, you could use @CompileStatic on a class that calculates the Fibonacci sequence:[3]

```
1    import    groovy.transform.*
2    @CompileStatic
3    class Foo {
4        void getFibs(int count) {
5            def list = [0, 1] // print first #count Fibonacci numbers
6            count.times {
7                print "${list.last()}"
8                list << list.sum()
9                list = list.tail()
10           }
11       }
12   }
```

✏️ **Exercise**   Try using @TypeChecked and the def keyword. It works surprisingly well.

Elvis Operator

The elvis operator was born from a common idiom in Java: using the ternary operation to provide a default value. For example:

```
1    String name = person.getName() == null ? "Bob" :    person.
     getName();
```

---

[3]https://en.wikipedia.org/wiki/Fibonacci_number

Instead in Groovy you can just use the elvis operator:

```
1   String name = person.getName() ?: "Bob"
```

Safe Dereference Operator

Similar to the elvis operator, Groovy has the safe dereference operator that allows you to easily avoid null-pointer exceptions. It involves simply adding a question mark. For example:

```
1   String name = person?.getName()
```

This would simply set name to null if person is null. It also works for method calls.

✏️ **Tip**   Write some Groovy code using the elvis operators and safe dereference several times until you memorize the syntax.

A Brief History

What follows is a brief history of updates to the Groovy language starting with Groovy 1.8. This will help you if you must use an older version of Groovy or if you haven't looked at Groovy in several years.

Groovy 1.8

- Command chains—The code "pull request on github" is executed as: pull(request).on(github)

- GPars[4] Bundled for parallel and concurrent paradigms (it was later pulled out)

---

[4]https://github.com/GPars/GPars

- Closure annotation parameters— `@Invariant({number >= 0})`

- Closure memorization—`{...}.memoize()`

- Built-in JSON support—Consuming, producing, and pretty-printing

- New AST transformations—`@Log, @Field, @AutoClone, @AutoExternalizable, ...`

Groovy 1.8 further improved the ability to omit unnecessary punctuation by supporting *command chains,* which allow you to omit parentheses and dots for a chain of method calls.

Groovy 2.0

- Groovy became more modular, with many parts broken out into multiple jars.

- It added the ability to create your own module which allows you to add methods to existing classes (Extension modules[5]).

- `@CompileStatic`: Compiles your Groovy code to byte-code.

- `@TypeChecked`: Enforces compile time type-checking (as seen in the previous section).

- Java 7 alignments: Try-with-resources, underscores in numeric literals, and invoke dynamic (optionally using the `-indy command option`).

---

[5]`http://docs.groovy-lang.org/latest/html/documentation/core-metaprogramming.html#_extension_modules`

- Java 7 multi-catch: `catch (Exception1 | Exception2 e) {}`

The huge change in Groovy 2 was the addition of the `@CompileStatic` and `@TypeChecked` annotations, which were already covered.

Groovy 2.1

- Full support for the JDK 7 "invoke dynamic" instruction and API.

- `@DelegatesTo`—A special annotation for closure delegate based DSLs and static type-checker extensions.

- Compile-time meta-annotations— `@groovy.transform.AnnotationCollector` can be used to create a meta-annotation.

- Many improvements to existing AST transformations.

This release saw a huge improvement in performance by taking advantage of Java 7's invoke dynamic. However, it is not enabled by default (this will be covered in a later chapter; basically you just have to "turn it on").

Groovy 2.2

- Implicit closure coercion.

- `@Memoized` AST transformation for methods.

- Bintray's JCenter repository.

- Define base script classes with an annotation.

- New `DelegatingScript` base class for scripts.

- @DelegatesTo with generic-type tokens.

- Precompiled type-checking extensions.

The main point to notice here is implicit closure coercion, which allows you to use closures anywhere a SAM (single abstract method) interface could be used. Before this release, you needed to cast the closure explicitly.

Groovy 2.3

- Official support for running Groovy on JDK 8

- Traits

- New and updated AST transformations

This release added a brand new concept (*traits*) and the `trait` keyword. We will cover them in a later chapter.

Groovy 2.4

- Android support

- Performance improvements and reduced byte-code

- Traits @Self Type annotation

- GDK improvements

- More AST transformations

Outdoing themselves yet again, the developers behind Groovy made tons of improvements and included Android support.

Groovy 2.5

Groovy 2.5 added support for JDK9+, added 11 new AST transformations, and added the macro feature which makes writing AST transformations much easier.

The annotations added in Groovy 2.5 include @AutoFinal, @AutoImplement, @ImmutableBase, @ImmutableOptions, @MapConstructor, @NamedDelegate, @NamedParam, @NamedParams, @NamedVariant, @PropertyOptions, and @VisibilityOptions.

Some of these annotations are described as follows:

- *@AutoImplement*: Automatically implements missing abstract methods (such as those from an interface). You can specify an exception to throw from those methods, such as UnsupportedOperationException. It can be useful for generating test stubs or when you only need to implement a subset of inherited abstract methods.

- *@AutoFinal*: Automatically adds final modifier to method parameters.

- *@MapConstructor*: Adds a constructor to your class that has one map parameter, expects field names as keys, and sets the corresponding field values. For example:

```
@groovy.transform.MapConstructor
class Person { String firstName; String lastName }
// later on...
def p= new Person(firstName: 'Peter', lastName: 'Quill')
assert p.firstName == 'Peter'
```

Also many annotations were improved with additional attributes. For example, @TupleConstructor now includes seven more attributes. The @Immutable annotation was updated to recognize that the date/time classes added in Java 8 are immutable, and to handle Optional.

Groovy 2.6

The 2.6 version of Groovy was going to be much like Groovy 3 without the need for JDK 8, but it was retired to focus on faster delivery of Groovy 3.0.

Groovy 3.0

Groovy 3.0 sports a completely rewritten parser (nicknamed *Parrot*) that brings Groovy up to parity with the latest Java 11 syntax along with new Groovy-only features. It runs on JDK 8 minimum and has better support for JDK 9/10/11.

The Java-like syntax now includes Java 8 style lambda expressions and method references and some tricky syntax which has eluded Groovy for many years: array initialization, do/while loops, commas in loop declarations, and some others.

New Operators

Identity

The operator "===" can now be used to express identity-equal and !== to mean not identity-equal. Since Groovy interprets == as ".equals", it used ".is" for identity-equals in the past. The support of "===" should avoid some confusion. This is similar to JavaScript's === operator.

Negative variants of operators

The new operator !instanceof and !in are now supported. This will simplify the syntax in these situations. Before you would have to type !(x instanceof Date), whereas now you can simply type x !instanceof Date. Likewise, for testing negative set inclusion, what used to be !(x in [1,2,3]) can now be written as x !in [1,2,3].

Elvis assignment

You may be familiar with the elvis operator (?:) in Groovy. In many cases you would use this operation to provide a default when assigning a value. For example, name = name ?: 'None'. Now you can shorten this expression to have the same meaning in Groovy 3 with the following: name ?= 'None'

Safe indexing

Much like the safe-reference operator, there is now a safe-indexing operator, ?. This allows you to access an index of an array (or list), but if the array is null, it will return null instead of throwing an exception. For example, the following would set the value to the first value of the array, or null if the array is null: value = array?[0]

Java parity

Groovy 3 support new features added from Java 8 to 11, such as lambda expressions, method references, constructor references, try-with-resources, code blocks, non-static inner classes, and even local variables (var).

All flavors of lambda expressions are supported (and compiled to closures unless you use @CompileStatic):

- No parameters—() -> expression

- Single parameter—x -> expression

- Explicit return is optional—(x, y) -> { x * y }

- Types are allowed—(int x, int y) -> { return x + y }

- Default values are allowed—(int x, int y = 10) -> x+y

Groovy has had method references for a long time, but Groovy 3 adds support for the Java 8+ syntax using the double colon. For example, the following is valid Groovy:

```
def sq(x) { x*x }
// var is similar to def
var squares = (1..9).collect( this::sq ) //method ref
//prints squares=[1, 4, 9, 16, 25, 36, 49, 64, 81]
```

Groovy 3 also implements the try-with-resources:

```
def f = new File('temp')
try (PrintWriter pw = new PrintWriter(f)) {
    pw.println("TEST!")
}
```

This would result in the file name "temp" having the contents "TEST!" and would automatically close the PrintWriter whether or not there were errors.

Summary

In this chapter, you learned about the following:

- How Groovy extends and simplifies programming on the JDK in a familiar syntax.

- Groovy's dynamic def, easy properties, closures, better "switch," meta-programming, type-checking and static-compile annotations, the elvis operator, and safe dereference.

- A brief overview of the features available to Groovy and in what versions they were introduced.

- How Groovy 3.0 brings Groovy up to date with Java's latest syntax as well as supporting some additional Java syntax that was not supported before.

CHAPTER 3

Tools

In addition to groovy, the Groovy installation comes with several helpful tools, covered in this chapter.

Console

```
1    groovyConsole
```

The Groovy Console is a quick and easy way to try things in Groovy visually without the overhead of a complete IDE.

Whenever you have an idea you want to try out quickly, open the Groovy Console, type some code, and then press Ctrl+R to run it. After reading your output and changing the code, press Ctrl+W to clear the output and Ctrl+R again to run the code. Once you get used to those two shortcuts, the Groovy Console might become an indispensable development tool.

It also has the ability (among other things) to inspect the AST (Abstract Syntax Tree) of your code, the internal representation of the code used by the compiler. Use `Script - Inspect Ast` or Ctrl+T to open the Groovy AST Browser.

You can provide a classpath to be available at runtime to the Groovy Console using the -cp option. This is useful when you want to refer to other classes you have compiled. For example, in a Linux/OSX environment, you use the following (where ":" is used to separate paths):

```
1   groovyConsole -cp src/main/groovy/:src/main/resources/
    example.groovy
```

Compilation

```
1   groovyc
```

Much like javac, groovyc compiles Groovy code to JVM byte-code (*.class files). It is not strictly necessary to compile before running. You can use the groovy command to run a groovy script file which typically end in .groovy but can have any extension.

To take advantage of the JDK 7+ invoke-dynamic instruction, use the --indy flag.[1] This also works with the groovy command.

Invoke-dynamic helps the compiler improve the performance of things like duck-typing, meta-programming, and method-missing calls.

Shell

```
1   groovysh
```

The Groovy shell can be used to execute Groovy code in an interactive command shell.

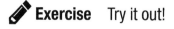 **Exercise**   Try it out!

---

[1]Available in Groovy 2.0 and above.

Documentation

```
1    groovydoc
```

This tool generates documentation from your Groovy code.

Groovy uses the same comment syntax as Java, including the conventions for documenting code.

```
1    /** This is a documentation comment. */
2    /* This is not */
3    // This is a one-line comment.
```

Groovy docs can even be accessed as metadata using the groovy.attach.groovydoc command line option.[2] For example, using the following at the command line:

```
groovyc -Dgroovy.attach.groovydoc=true Test.groovy
```

Given that you put the following code in Test.groovy:

```
/** My class */ class Test { /** My method */ def method() {} }
```

You could access those documents from the AST at compile time (this can be useful when writing AST transformations, for example).

Also, Groovy docs can be accessed at runtime using the groovy.attach.runtime.groovydoc command line option. For example, using the following at the command line:

```
groovyc -Dgroovy.attach.runtime.groovydoc=true Test.groovy
```

Given the following code in "Test.groovy":

```
class Test { /**@ My metadata */ def method() {} }
```

---

[2]Available in Groovy 3.0 and beyond.

You can now access the preceding comment metadata using the following code (in Groovy 3):

```
def data = Test.methods.find{ it.name=='method' }.groovydoc.content
assert data == 'My metadata'
```

CHAPTER 4

GDK

The GDK (Groovy Development Kit) provides a number of helper methods, operators, utilities, and additional classes.

Some of these are methods added to every Java class, like "each", and some are more obscure.

Collections

Groovy adds tons of helpful methods that allow easier manipulation of collections, arrays, or any `Iterable`:

- sort—Sorts the collection (if it is sortable).

- findAll—Finds all elements that match a closure.

- collect—An iterator that builds a new collection.

- inject—Loops through the values and returns a single value (similar to the concept of "reduce").

- each—Iterates through the values using the given closure.

- eachWithIndex—Iterates through with two parameters: a value and an index.

- find—Finds the first element that returns true when passed to a given a closure.

© Adam L. Davis 2019
A. L. Davis, *Learning Groovy 3*, https://doi.org/10.1007/978-1-4842-5058-7_4

- findIndexOf—Finds the first element that matches a closure and returns its index.

- any—True if any element returns true for the closure (like OR).

- every—True if all elements return true for the closure (like AND).

- reverse—Reverses the ordering of elements in a list.

- first—Gets the first element of a list.

- last—Returns the last element of a list.

- tail—Returns all elements except the first element of a list (useful for, e.g., recursive strategies).

Java 8 Streams

Groovy adds support to simplify dealing with Java 8+ Streams as well. For example, toList() and toSet() are added to the java.util.stream. Stream<T> interface allowing you to shortcut collect(Collectors. toList()) and collect(Collectors.toSet()), respectively.

Spread

The spread operator can be used to access the property of every element in a collection. It can be used instead of collect in many cases. For example, let's take a simple Dragon class defined as follows:

```
class Dragon { String name }
```

You could print the name of every Dragon in a list named dragons:

```
1   dragons*.name.each { println it }
```

This is a shorter form for the following:

```
1    dragons.collect { dragon -> d.name }.each { println it }
```

GPath

GPath is something like XPath in Groovy. Thanks to the support of property notation for both lists and maps, Groovy provides syntactic sugar, making it really easy to deal with nested collections, as illustrated in the following examples:

```
1    def listOfMaps = [['a': 11, 'b': 12], ['a': 21, 'b': 22]]
2    assert listOfMaps.a == [11, 21] //GPath notation
3    assert listOfMaps*.a == [11, 21] //spread dot notation
4
5    listOfMaps = [['a': 11, 'b': 12], ['a': 21, 'b': 22], null]
6    assert listOfMaps*.a == [11, 21, null]
     // caters for null values
7    assert listOfMaps*.a == listOfMaps.collect { it?.a }
     //equivalent notation
8    // But this will only collect non-null values
9    assert listOfMaps.a == [11,21]
```

As demonstrated in the preceding examples, *. provides null values, whereas using only "." skips any null values.

IO

The GDK helps you a lot with input/output (IO).

Files

The GDK adds several methods to the File class to ease reading and writing files.

```
1   println path.toFile().text
```

A getText() method is added to the File class, which simply reads the whole file.

```
1   new  File("books.txt").text = "Modern Java"
```

Here we are using the setText method on the File class, which simply writes the file contents. For binary files, you can also use the bytes property on File:

```
1   byte[] data = new   File('data').bytes
2   new  File('out').bytes = data
```

If you want to use an InputStream or reader or the corresponding OutputStream or writer for output, you have the following methods which also handle closing the stream for you:

```
1   new File('dragons.txt').withInputStream {in -> }
2   new  File('dragons.txt').withReader {r -> }
3   new  File('dragons.txt').withOutputStream {out ->}
4   new  File('dragons.txt').withWriter {w -> }
```

Lastly you can use the eachLine method to read each line of a file. For example:

```
1   new  File('dragons.txt').eachLine { line->
2     println "$line"
3   }
4   //OR
5   new  File('dragons.txt').eachLine { line, num ->
```

```
6     println "Line $num: $line"
7   }
```

In all of these cases, Groovy takes care of closing the I/O resource even if an exception is thrown.

✎ **Exercise**   Print out a multiline file and then read it back in and print out the lines.

URLs

The GDK makes it extremely simple to execute a URL.

The following Java code opens an HTTP connection on the given URL (http://google.com in this case), reads the data into a byte array, and prints out the resulting text.

```
1    URL url = new  URL("http://google.com");
2    InputStream input = (InputStream) url.getContent();
3    ByteArrayOutputStream out = new  ByteArrayOutputStream();
4    int n = 0;
5    byte[] arr = new byte[1024];
6
7    while  (-1 != (n = input.read(arr)))
8    out.write(arr, 0, n);
9
10   System.out.println(new String(out.toByteArray()));
```

However, in Groovy this also can be reduced to one line (leaving out exceptions):

```
1    println "http://google.com".toURL().text
```

A toURL() method is added to the String class, and a getText() method (which is called using ".text") is added to the URL class in Groovy.

✏️ **Exercise**   Use Groovy to download your favorite web site and see if you can parse something from it.

Ranges

The Range is a built-in type in Groovy. It can be used to perform loops, in switch cases, extracting substrings, and other places. Ranges are generally defined using the syntax start..end.

Ranges come in handy for traversing using the each method and for loops:

```
1   (1..4).each {print it} //1234
2   for (i in 1..4) print i //1234
```

A case statement was demonstrated in an earlier chapter, such as the following:

```
switch (x) {
        case "foo": result = "foo"
            break
        case  12..30: result = "12 to 30"
            break
```

⚠️ **Warning**   This works only if the value given to the switch statement is the same type as the Range (an Integer in this case).

You can use ranges to extract substrings from a string using the getAt syntax. For example:

```
1   def text = 'learning groovy',
2   println text[0..4] //learn
3   println text[0..4, 8..-1] //learn groovy
```

🔑 **Tip**   Negative numbers count down from the last element of a collection or string. So -1 equates to the last element.

You can also use ranges to access elements of a list:

```
1   def list = ['hank', 'john', 'fred']
2   println list[0..1] //[hank, john]
```

You can define a range to be exclusive of the last number by using the ..< operator. For example, another way to print 1234 would be the following:

```
1   (1..<5).each {print it} //1234
```

✏️ **Exercise**   Attempt to use a variable in a range. Do you need to surround the variable with parentheses?

Utilities

The GDK adds several utility classes, such as ConfigSlurper, JsonBuilder, JsonSlurper, Expando, and ObservableList/Map/Set.

ConfigSlurper

ConfigSlurper is a utility class for reading configuration files defined in the form of Groovy scripts. Like with Java Properties files (files ending with .properties), ConfigSlurper allows for a dot notation. It also allows for nested (closure) configuration values and arbitrary object types.

```
1   def config = new ConfigSlurper().parse('''
2       app.date = new Date()
3       app.age  = 42
4       app {
5           name = "Test${42}"
6       }
7   ''')
8
9   def properties = config.toProperties()
10
11  assert properties."app.date" instanceof String
12  assert properties."app.age" == '42'
13  assert properties."app.name" == 'Test42'
```

JsonBuilder and JsonSlurper

Groovy has the JsonBuilder and JsonSlurper classes to help deal with JSON (JavaScript Object Notation), a very common data format. They both are in the "groovy.json" package. For example:

```
import groovy.json.*
def builder = new JsonBuilder()
builder.person {
    name 'Adam'
    age 37
```

```
    conferences 'Gr8Conf', 'ÜberConf'
}
println builder
```

The preceding code demonstrates using the JsonBuilder to build a person object which would result in the following output:

```
{"person":{"name":"Adam","age":37,"conferences":["Gr8Conf","
ÜberConf"]}
```

Likewise we can use the JsonSlurper to parse JSON as follows:

```
def slurper = new JsonSlurper()
def result = slurper.parseText(builder.toString())
assert result.person.name == "Adam"
assert result.person.age == 37
assert result.person.conferences.size() == 2
assert result.person.conferences[0] == "Gr8Conf"
```

This parses the same JSON from the previously defined builder and verifies that the returned values are as expected. Note that "result" is a map of values, "person" is also a map, and "conferences" is a list in this case.

Expando

The Expando class can be used to create a dynamically expandable object. You can add fields and methods. This can be useful when you want to use extremely dynamic meta-programming. For example, see the following code:

```
1    def expando = new Expando()
2    expando.name = 'Draco' // field value
3    expando.say = { String s -> "${name} says $s" } //method
4    expando.say('hello') // Output: Draco says hello
```

✏ **Exercise**   Use meta-programming to alter some class's
`metaClass` and then print out the class of the `metaClass`. Is it the
Expando class?

ObservableList/Map/Set

Groovy comes with observable lists, maps, and sets. Each of these collections
triggers `PropertyChangeEvent` (from the `java.beans` package) when
elements are added, removed, or changed. Note that a `PropertyChangeEvent`
does not only signal that an event has occurred, it also holds information on
the property name and the old/new value of a property.

Here's an example using `ObservableList` and printing out the class of
each event:

```
1   def list = new ObservableList()
2   def printer = {e -> println e.class}
3   list.addPropertyChangeListener(printer)
4   list.add 'Harry Potter'
5   list.add 'Hermione Granger'
6   list.remove(0)
7   println list
```

This would result in the following output:

```
1   class groovy.util.ObservableList$ElementAddedEvent
2   class java.beans.PropertyChangeEvent
3   class groovy.util.ObservableList$ElementAddedEvent
4   class java.beans.PropertyChangeEvent
5   class groovy.util.ObservableList$ElementRemovedEvent
6   class java.beans.PropertyChangeEvent
7   [Hermione Granger]
```

This can be useful for using the `Observer` pattern on collections.

✎ **Exercise**   Use an `ObservableMap` and a `PropertyChangeListener` to reject null values from being added to the map.

CHAPTER 5

Coming from Java

Since most readers are already familiar with Java, it would be helpful to compare common Java idioms with the Groovy equivalent.

Default Method Values

One thing that might surprise you coming from Java is that in Groovy you can provide default values for method parameters. For example, let's say you have a `fly` method with a parameter called `text`:

```
1   def fly(String text = "flying") {println text}
```

Note   Using the "def" keyword in this way defines a method with return type of `java.lang.Object`.

This would essentially create two methods behind the scenes (from a Java standpoint):

```
1   def  fly() {println "flying"}
2   def  fly(String text) {println text}
```

© Adam L. Davis 2019
A. L. Davis, *Learning Groovy 3*, https://doi.org/10.1007/978-1-4842-5058-7_5

This can work with any number of parameters as long as the resulting methods do not conflict with other existing methods. Given our preceding example, we can test it as follows:

```
fly() // output: flying
fly('Groovy') // output: Groovy
```

Equals, HashCode, and More

Groovy has many annotations in the "groovy.transform" package that implement **AST transformations** (Abstract Syntax Tree transformations). In other words, they simplify life by adding commonly written code (often called "boilerplate") to the byte-code of your class for you at compilation time when you use them to annotate your class.

One of the tedious tasks you must often do in Java is create an equals and a hashCode method for a class. For this purpose, Groovy added the @EqualsAndHashCode annotation. Simply add it to the top of your class (right before the word class) and you're done.

Likewise, you often want to create a constructor for all of the fields of a class. For this, Groovy has @TupleConstructor. It uses the order of the definitions of your fields to define a constructor with parameters for initializing those fields. Just add it right before your class definition.

There's also the @ToString annotation you can add before your class definition for automatically creating a toString() method for your class. You can also configure it to include or exclude certain fields.

Finally, if you want to have all of these things on your class, just use the @Canonical annotation. You can use Ctrl+T in the groovyConsole to see how this affects the syntax tree.

```
1   import groovy.transform.*
2   @Canonical class Dragon {def name}
3   println new Dragon("Smaug")
```

```
4    // prints: Dragon(Smaug)
5    assert new Dragon("").equals(new Dragon(""))
```

✏️ **Exercise**   Create your own class with multiple properties using these annotations.

Regex Pattern Matching

Groovy greatly simplifies using a pattern to match text using regex (regular expressions).

Where in Java you must use the `java.util.regex.Pattern` class, create an instance, and then create a Matcher; in Groovy this can all be simplified to one line.

By convention you surround your regex with slashes. This allows you to use special regex syntax without using the tedious double backslash. For example, to determine if a String is an e-mail address (given a variable named `email`):

```
1    def  isEmail = email ==~ /[\w.]+@[\w.]+/
```

The equivalent code in Java would be

```
1    Pattern patt = Pattern.compile("[\\w.]+@[\\w.]+");
2    boolean  isEmail = patt.matches(email);
```

There's also an operator for creating a matcher in Groovy:

```
1    def email = 'mailto:adam@email.com'
2    def  mr = email =~ /[\w.]+@[\w.]+/
3    if (mr.find()) println mr.group()
```

This allows you to find regular expressions inside strings and to get sub-groups from a regex.

45

Exercise   Create a better regex for validating e-mail in Groovy.

Missing Java Syntax

Due to the nature of Groovy's syntax and some additions to Java's syntax over the years, Groovy was "missing" a few things before version 3.0. However, there are other ways to do the same things.

Arrays can be somewhat difficult to work with in Groovy pre-3.0 because the Java syntax for creating an array of values does not compile. For example, the following would not compile in Groovy 2.5:

```
1   String[] array = new  String[] {"foo", "bar"};
```

You should instead use the following syntax (if you must use an array):

```
1   String[] array = ['foo', 'bar'].toArray()
```

There are several options in Groovy for iterating through a list, array, or collection: using the in keyword, the Java style, or the each method with a closure. For example:

```
1   for (String item : array) println(item)
2   for (item in array) println(item)
3   array.each { item -> println(item) }
```

Optional Semicolon

Since the semicolon is optional in Groovy, this can sometimes cause line-ending confusion when you're used to Java. Usually this is not a problem, but when calling multiple methods in a row (using a fluent API, for example), this can cause problems. In this case, you need to end each line with a non-closed operator, such as a dot.

For example, let's take an arbitrary fluent API:

```
1  class Pie  {
2    def  bake() { this }
3    def  make() { this }
4    def  eat() { this }
5  }
6  def pie = new Pie().
7          make().
8          bake().
9          eat()
```

If you were to use the typical Java syntax, it might cause a compilation error in older versions Groovy (not true anymore):

```
1  def pie = new Pie() //Groovy interprets end of line
2          .make() // huh? what is this?
```

Optional Parenthesis Sometimes

Groovy allows parenthesis to be left out in some cases to simplify the syntax. The two main cases are as follows: when making a method call with one or more parameters and when a closure is the last (or only) parameter. For example, the following would work in Groovy:

```
1  // call a method named "doStuff" with parameter 1
2  doStuff 1
3  // call "doStuff" with three parameters:
4  doStuff 1, 2, 3
5  // call "each" on "list" with one Closure:
6  list.each { item -> doStuff(item) }
```

Where Are Generics?

Groovy supports the syntax of generics but does not enforce them by default. For this reason, you might not see a lot of generics in Groovy code. For example, the following would work fine in Groovy:

```
1   List<Integer> nums = [1, 2, 3.1415, 'pie']
```

However, Groovy will enforce generics if you add the @CompileStatic or @TypeChecked annotation to your class or method. For example:

```
1   import groovy.transform.*
2   @CompileStatic
3   class Foo {
4       List<Integer> nums = [1, 2, 3.1415] //error
5   }
```

This would cause the compilation error "[Static type checking] - Incompatible generic argument types. Cannot assign java.util. List <java.lang.Number> to: java.util.List <Integer>". Since 3.1415 becomes a java.math.BigDecimal in Groovy, the generic type of the list is automatically determined to be java.lang.Number.

Groovy Numbers

This discussion leads us to decimal numbers, which use BigDecimal by default in Groovy. This allows you to do math without rounding errors.

If you want to use double or float, simply follow your number with d or f, respectively (as you can also do in Java). For example:

```
1   def  pie = 3.141592d
```

✎ **Exercise**   Try multiplying different number types and determining the class of the result.

Boolean-Resolution

Since Groovy is very similar to Java, but not Java, it's easy to get confused by the differences. A couple of the areas of confusion are *boolean-resolution* (also called "Groovy truth") and the *Map syntax sugar*.

Groovy is much more liberal in what it accepts in a Boolean expression. For example, null, an empty Collection, an empty String, and a zero are considered false. So, the following prints out "true" four times:

```
1   if ("foo") println("true")
2   if (!"") println("true")
3   if (42) println("true")
4   if (! 0) println("true")
```

🔑 **Tip**   This is sometimes referred to as "Groovy truth".

Map Syntax

Groovy syntax sugar for maps allows you use string keys directly, which is often very helpful. However, this can cause confusion when attempting to get the class-type of a map using Groovy's property-accessor syntax sugar (.class refers to the key-value, not getClass()). So you should use the getClass() method directly.

This can also cause confusion when you're trying to use variables as keys. In this case, you need to surround the variables with parentheses. For example:

```
1   def foo = "key"
2   def bar = 2
3   def map = [(foo): bar]
```

Without the parentheses, foo would resolve to the String "foo". With the parentheses, the String "key" will be used as the key mapped to the value 2.

Summary

In this chapter, you learned about the following Groovy features:

- You can provide default method values.

- Various annotations that simplify life in the groovy.transform package.

- How regular expressions are built into Groovy.

- Different ways of defining arrays in Groovy.

- How to use unclosed operations when writing a multiline statement.

- Groovy uses BigDecimal by default for non-integer numbers.

- Groovy truth.

- You can use variable keys in the map syntax.

PART II

Advanced Groovy

Beyond the basics, Groovy is a rich tapestry of language features. It can be used either dynamically or statically typed; it's your choice. It supports functional programming constructs, including first-class functions, method references, currying, and more. It has multiple inheritance, type inference, and meta-programming.

CHAPTER 6

Groovy Design Patterns

Design patterns are a great way to make your code functional, readable, and extensible. There are some patterns that are easier and require less code in Groovy compared to Java.

Strategy Pattern

Imagine you have three different methods for finding totals as follows:

```
1    def totalPricesLessThan10(prices) {
2            int total = 0
3            for (int price : prices)
4                    if (price < 10) total += price
5            total
6    }
7      def totalPricesMoreThan10(prices) {
8            int total = 0
9            for (int price : prices)
10                    if (price > 10) total += price
11            total
12    }
13    def   totalPrices(prices) {
14            int total = 0
```

© Adam L. Davis 2019
A. L. Davis, *Learning Groovy 3*, https://doi.org/10.1007/978-1-4842-5058-7_6

```
15              for (int price : prices)
16                      total += price
17          total
18  }
```

A lot of code is duplicated in this case. There's only one small thing that changes in each of these methods. In Groovy, you can use a closure parameter instead of three different methods so you can have the following:

```
1   def totalPrices(prices, selector) {
2          int total = 0
3          for (int price : prices)
4                  if (selector(price)) total += price
5          total
6   }
```

Now you have a method, totalPrices(prices, selector), where selector is a closure. Also, you can put the closure outside of the method parameters in a method call if it's the last parameter. So you can call this method in the following ways to achieve the desired results:

```
1   totalPrices(prices) { it < 10 }
2   totalPrices(prices) { it > 10 }
3   totalPrices(prices) { true }
```

This not only makes your code more concise, it's also easier to read and extend.

Meta-Programming

Groovy meta-programming means you can add functionality (fields and methods) to any class or interface at runtime. This allows you to add helper methods to commonly used classes or interfaces to make your code more concise and readable.

Meta-Class

You can add commonly used functionality using the metaClass in a dynamic Groovy project (without using @CompileStatic or @TypeChecked). For example, if you often need to split text into words, you could add a method to the String class using the following code:

```
String.metaClass.words = { -> split(/ +/) }
def text = "the lazy brown fox"
text.words() // Result: ['the', 'lazy', 'brown', 'fox']
```

For another example, let's say you're writing a javax.servlet.Filter and you get and set session attributes a lot. You could do the following to virtually add methods to the HttpSession interface:

```
1  HttpSession.metaClass.getAt = { key -> getAttribute(key) }
2  HttpSession.metaClass.putAt = {
3      key, value -> setAttribute(key, value)
4  }
```

This allows the following syntax for setting and getting attributes of your session:

```
1  def  session = request.session
2  session['my_id'] = '123' // calls putAt('my_id', '123')
3  def  id = session['my_id'] // calls getAt('my_id')
```

Categories

Category is one of the many meta-programming techniques available in Groovy. A Category is a class that can be used to add functionality to existing classes. It can be useful when you don't want to mess with a class for the whole application, but only want special treatment for a limited section of the code.

To make a Category, you create some static methods that have at least one parameter of a particular type (e.g., an integer). When the Category is used, that type (the type of the first parameter) appears to have those methods in addition to its previously defined methods. The object instance on which the method is called is used as the first parameter.

For example, Groovy has the TimeCategory[1] Category built-in for manipulating dates and times. This lets you add and subtract any arbitrary length of time. For example:

```
1   import groovy.time.TimeCategory
2   def now = new Date()
3   println now
4   use(TimeCategory) {
5       nextWeekPlusTenHours = now + 1.week + 10.hours
6   }
7   println nextWeekPlusTenHours
```

In this case, TimeCategory adds a bunch of methods to the Integer class. For example, some of the method signatures look like the following:

```
1   static Duration getDays(Integer self)
2   static TimeDuration getHours(Integer self)
3   static TimeDuration getMinutes(Integer self)
4   static DatumDependentDuration getMonths(Integer self)
5   static TimeDuration getSeconds(Integer self)
```

✏️ **Exercise**   Create your own Category class and then put it on GitHub.

---

[1]http://docs.groovy-lang.org/latest/html/api/groovy/time/TimeCategory.html

Missing Methods

In Groovy you can intercept missing methods (methods that are called, but are not defined in the classic sense) using the methodMissing method. This can be a very useful design pattern when you want to dynamically define methods at runtime with a flexible method name and signature. You write the methodMissing signature as follows:

```
1   def methodMissing(String name, args) { /* your code */ }
```

The name parameter is the name of the missing method, and the args parameter is all of the arguments passed to that method (as an object array). You then can write whatever functionality you want this method to have, using the name and args parameters.

Next, to improve efficiency, you can intercept, cache, and invoke the called method. For example:

```
1   def methodMissing(String name, args) {
2           def impl = { /* your code */ }
3           getMetaClass()."$name" = impl
4           impl()
5   }
```

This implements the missing functionality and then adds it to the current class's metaClass so that future calls go directly to the implementation instead of the methodMissing method. This might be useful if you expect the same missing methods to be called a lot.

To test this out, let's implement a very simple method that just prints out the called method name:

```
def methodMissing(String name, args) {
    println "in methodMissing"
    def impl = { println name }
```

```
    getMetaClass()."$name" = impl
    impl()
}
```

Now we can call missing methods like the following:

```
wow()
thisworks()
wow()
```

The output shown below demonstrates that the second call to "wow" uses the metaClass method, not methodMissing:

```
in methodMissing
wow
in methodMissing
thisworks
wow
```

Delegation

Delegation is when a class has methods that directly call (method signature identical) methods of another class. This is hard in Java because it is difficult and time consuming to add methods to a class.

This is much easier with the @Delegate annotation. It's like compile-time meta-programming. It automatically adds the methods of the delegate class to the current class.

For example:

```
1    public class Person {
2            def  eatDonuts() { println("yummy") }
3    }
4
```

```
5   public class RoboCop {
6           @Delegate final Person person
7
8           public RoboCop(Person person) { this.person =
            person }
9           public RoboCop() { this.person = new Person() }
10
11          def crushCars() {
12                  println("smash")
13          }
14  }
```

Although RoboCop does not have an eatDonuts() method, all of the methods of Person are added to RoboCop and delegated to person. This allows for the following usage:

```
1   def  person = new  RoboCop()
2   person.eatDonuts()
3   person.crushCars()
```

✏ **Exercise**   Use @Delegate on a List property and use it to make a list that cannot have elements removed.

CHAPTER 7

DSLs

Groovy has many features that make it great for writing DSLs (domain-specific languages):

- Closures with delegates.

- Parentheses and dots (.) are optional (command chains).

- Ability to add methods to standard classes using Categories and Extension modules.

- The ability to override many operators (plus, minus, etc.).

- The `methodMissing` and `propertyMissing` methods.

Domain-specific languages can be useful for many purposes, such as allowing domain experts to read and write code or to clarify the meaning of business logic. They allow business experts to read or write code without having to be programming experts.

Closure with Delegate

Within Groovy you can take a block of code (a closure) as a parameter and then call it using a local variable as a delegate. For example, imagine you have the following code for sending SMS texts:

```
1    class SMS {
2            String from, to, body;
3            def  from(String fromNumber) {
```

© Adam L. Davis 2019
A. L. Davis, *Learning Groovy 3*, https://doi.org/10.1007/978-1-4842-5058-7_7

```
4                          from = fromNumber
5                  }
6                  def  to(String toNumber) {
7                          to = toNumber
8                  }
9                  def  body(String body) {
10                         this.body = body
11                 }
12                 def  send() {
13                         // send the text.
14                 }
15     }
```

In Java, you'd need to use this the following way:

```
1   SMS m = new  SMS();
2   m.from("555-432-1234");
3   m.to("555-678-4321");
4   m.body("Hey there!");
5   m.send();
```

In Groovy you can add the following static method to the SMS class for DSL-like usage (block is expected to be a closure):

```
1   def static send(@DelegatesTo(SMS) Closure block) {
2           SMS m = new  SMS()
3           block.delegate = m
4           block()
5           m.send()
6   }
```

This sets the SMS object as a delegate for the block so that methods are forwarded to it. The (optional) @DelegatesTo(SMS) annotation tells the compiler and IDE what class is used as delegate to the closure. Now you can do the following:

```
1   SMS.send {
2           from '555-432-1234'
3           to '555-678-4321'
4           body 'Hey there!'
5   }
```

This removes a lot of repetition from the code.

Tip   As demonstrated, you can omit the parentheses when making a simple method call.

Command Chains

As noted earlier, Groovy has support for *command chains* which allow you to completely omit parenthesis and dots when making method calls with one or more parameters.

For example, let's take the previous class for sending SMS messages but convert it to support the command chain syntax.

```
1   class SMS {
2           String from, to, body;
3           SMS  from(String fromNumber) {
4                   from = fromNumber; return this
5           }
6           SMS  to(String toNumber) {
7                   to = toNumber; return this
8           }
```

```
 9          SMS  body(String body) {
10                  this.body = body; return this
11          }
12          def  send() { /* send the text */ }
13          def static send(@DelegatesTo(SMS) Closure block) {
14          /* same as before */ }
15  }
```

Now our DSL syntax can be used like the following:

```
1   SMS.send {
3           from '555-432-1234' to '555-678-4321'
4               body 'Hey there!'
5   }
```

Overriding Operators

In Groovy you can override operators simply by naming your methods
using the English word for the operator. For example, plus for + and minus
for -. See the following table for more operators:

Operator	Method Name
+	plus
-	minus
*	multiply
/	div
%	mod
**	power
|	or

Operator	Method Name
&	and
^	xor
<<	leftShift
>>	rightShift
++	next
--	previous

For more complex operators, the variables "a", "b", and "c" are used to demonstrate how they are used in the following table (where "a" is an instance of the class defining the method):

Example	Method Declaration
a()	call()
a as b	asType(b)
a[b]	getAt(b)
a[b] = c	putAt(b,c)
+a	positive()
-a	negative()
~a	bitwiseNegate()
b in a	isCase(b)

For example, let's create a class called `Logic` with a Boolean value and define the and and or methods.

```
1   class  Logic  {
2       boolean value
3       Logic(v) {this.value = v}
4       def and(Logic other) {
5           this.value && other.value
6       }
7       def or(Logic other) {
8           this.value || other.value
9       }
10  }
```

Then, let's use these methods and see if they work like we would expect:

```
1   def  pale = new  Logic(true)
2   def old = new Logic(false)
3
4   println "groovy truth: ${pale && old}" //true
5   println "using and: ${pale & old}" // false
6   println "using or: ${pale | old}" // true
```

Notice that using the built-in && operator uses "Groovy truth" and returns true because both variables are non-null.

Next, let's try defining the `leftShift` and `minus` operators on a class:

```
1   class Wizards {
2       def list = []
3       def leftShift(person) { list.add person }
4       def  minus(person) { list.remove person }
5       String toString() { "Wizards: $list" }
6   }
```

```
7   def wiz = new Wizards()
8   wiz << 'Gandolf'
9   println wiz // Wizards: [Gandolf]
10  wiz << 'Harry'
11  println wiz // Wizards: [Gandolf, Harry]
12  wiz - 'Harry'
13  println wiz // Wizards: [Gandolf]
```

You can also implement the putAt and getAt methods that allow you to use the bracket syntax. For example:

```
1   def value = wiz[1] // uses getAt(1)
2   wiz[1] = value // uses putAt(1, value)
```

This can be useful when writing for a domain that uses the bracket notation.

Missing Methods and Properties

As noted previously, Groovy provides a way to implement functionality at runtime via the methodMissing method:

```
1   def methodMissing(String name, args)
```

However, Groovy also provides a way to intercept missing properties that are accessed using Groovy's property syntax. Property access is implemented using propertyMissing(String name) (which returns a value) and property modification via propertyMissing(String name, Object value) (which sets the value for a property).

For example, here's an excerpt from a DSL for chemical compounds:

```
1   class Chemistry {
2     public static void exec(Closure block) {
3       block.delegate = new Chemistry()
```

```
 4        block()
 5      }
 6      def propertyMissing(String name) {
 7        def  comp = new  Compound(name)
 8        (comp.elements.size() == 1 && comp.elements.values()
          [0]==1) ?
 9           comp.elements.keySet()[0] : comp
10      }
11    }
```

Given the following code for Compound and Element:

```
// Represents a chemical Element
class Element  {
    String symbol
    Element(s) { symbol = s }
    double getWeight() {symbol=='H' ? 1.00794 : 15.9994}
    String toString() { symbol }
}
// Represents a chemical Compound
class Compound {
    final Map elements = [:]
    Compound(String str) {
                def matcher = str =~ /([A-Z][a-z]*)([0-9]+)?/
            while (matcher.find()) add(
                    new Element(matcher.group(1)),
                    (matcher.group(2) ?: 1) as Integer)
    }
    void add(Element e, int num) {
         if (elements[e]) elements[e] += num
         else elements[e] = num
    }
```

```
double getWeight() {
    elements.keySet().inject(0d) { sum, key ->
                    sum + (key.weight * elements[key])
    }
}
String toString() { "$elements" }
}
```

In this example, propertyMissing (on lines 6-9) creates a new Compound object and returns either the Compound or an Element object if there is only one element in the Compound. This enables the creation of Compounds based on the name of a missing property. For example:

```
1   def  c = new  Chemistry()
2   def water = c.H2O
3   println water // [H: 2, O: 1]
4   println water.weight // 18.01528
```

This is interpreted as trying to access a property named H2O, which triggers the propertyMissing method.

ℹ️ Info   H2O refers to the chemical composition of water, which is two hydrogen atoms and one oxygen atom.

By using the static exec method, this DSL reaches its full potential by exposing an instance of Chemistry as a delegate to the closure, which allows for the following example:

```
1   Chemistry.exec {
2           def water = H2O
3           println water
4           println water.weight
5   }
```

This has the same effect of creating the H2O compound by calling the propertyMissing method of Chemistry.

The full code for Groovy Chemisty[1] is provided on GitHub. It provides the ability to compute the atomic weights of chemical compounds and percentages by atomic weight. It includes all known elements, their names, and atomic weights.

This DSL would be very difficult to implement without the help of Groovy. In Java, for example, you would need to use strings to represent compounds, polluting the syntax with tons of quotes and parentheses.

Extension Modules

Extension modules in Groovy allow you to add functionality to existing classes to a project by including a library. It works much like Categories but works everywhere without requiring a use clause.

To create an Extension module, create a file named org.codehaus. groovy.runtime.ExtensionModule under the META-INF/services/ directory. Within that file, list all of your extensionClasses and staticExtensionClasses. For example, create such a file with the following contents:

```
moduleName=adamldavis-groovy-dsl-example
moduleVersion=0.1-beta1
extensionClasses=com.adamldavis.gdsl.MyDSLExtension
staticExtensionClasses=com.adamldavis.gdsl.MyStaticDSLExtension
```

When included in a project, Groovy will look at all of the static methods of the MyDSLExtension class (in the com.adamldavis.gdsl package) and use them to add functionality to instances of the first parameter of each method's class. The moduleName and moduleVersion

---

[1]https://github.com/adamldavis/groovy-chemistry

properties are only there to make sure multiple conflicting versions of the library are not loaded.

For example, given the following code, the String class would essentially have the upper() method added to it.

```groovy
class MyDSLExtension {
    static String upper(String it) { it.toUpperCase() }
}
```

Likewise, Groovy will look at all of the static methods of the MyStaticDSLExtension class and use them to add functionality to the class of the first parameter of each method. For example, the following code would add a method, boom, to the String class allowing String.boom() to return "!":

```groovy
class MyStaticDSLExtension {
    static String boom(String it) { "!" }
}
```

Note that for staticExtensionClasses, the given parameter (it in the preceding code) cannot be used within the method; it is only used for the type.

✎ **Exercise**   Create a DSL in Groovy for something that interests you, be it sports, math, movies, or astrophysics.

CHAPTER 8

Traits

Traits are like interfaces with default implementations and state.

Those familiar with Java 8 know that it added the default methods feature to interfaces. Traits are similar to Java 8 interfaces but with the added ability to have state (fields). This allows more flexibility but should be treated with caution.

Defining Traits

A Trait is defined using the trait keyword:

```
1   trait Animal {
2       int hunger = 100
3       def  eat() { println "eating"; hunger -= 1 }
4       abstract int getNumberOfLegs()
5   }
```

As this code demonstrates, Traits can have properties, methods, and abstract methods. If a class implements a Trait, it must implement its abstract methods.

Using Traits

To use a Trait, you use the `implements` keyword. For example:

```
1   class Rocket  {
2       String name
3       def  launch() { println(name + "Take off!") }
4   }
5   trait MoonLander {
6       def land() { println("${getName()} Landing!") }
7       abstract String getName()
8   }
9   class  Apollo  extends  Rocket implements  MoonLander {
10  }
```

Note how the abstract getName() method is implemented automatically by Groovy since the Rocket class has the name property.

So now you can do the following:

```
1   def  apollo = new  Apollo(name: "Apollo 12")
2   apollo.launch()
3   apollo.land()
```

This would generate the following output:

```
1   Apollo 12 Take off!
2   Apollo 12 Landing!
```

Unlike super-classes, you can use multiple traits in one class. Here is such an example:

```
1   trait Shuttle {
2       boolean canFly() { true }
3       abstract int getCargoBaySize()
4   }
```

```
5   class MoonShuttle  extends  Rocket
6       implements  MoonLander, Shuttle {
7       int getCargoBaySize() { 100 }
8   }
```

This would allow you to do the following:

```
1   MoonShuttle m = new  MoonShuttle(name: 'Taxi')
2   println "${m.name} can fly? ${m.canFly()}"
3   println "cargo bay: ${m.getCargoBaySize()}"
4   m.launch()
5   m.land()
```

Given the predecing code, you would get the following output:

```
1   Taxi can fly? true
2   cargo bay: 100
3   Taxi Take off!
4   Taxi Landing!
```

✏️ **Exercise**   See what happens when you have the same fields or methods in two different traits and then try to mix them.

Summary

In this chapter, you learned about the following Groovy features:

- What Traits are, which is similar to Java 8 interfaces.

- How to define a Trait with fields and methods.

- How you can use multiple Traits in one class.

CHAPTER 9

Functional Programming

Functional Programming (FP) is a programming style that focuses on functions and minimizes changes of state (using immutable data structures). It is closer to expressing solutions mathematically rather than step-by-step instructions.

In FP, functions should be "side-effect free" (nothing outside the function is changed) and *referentially transparent* (a function returns the same value every time when given the same arguments).

FP can be seen as an alternative to the more common *imperative programming,* which is closer to telling the computer the steps to follow.

Although functional-programming can be achieved in pre-Java 8,[1] Java 8 enabled language-level FP support with lambda expressions and *functional interfaces.*

Java 8, JavaScript, Groovy, and Scala all support functional-style programming, although they are not strictly FP languages.

---

[1]http://functionaljava.org/

© Adam L. Davis 2019
A. L. Davis, *Learning Groovy 3*, https://doi.org/10.1007/978-1-4842-5058-7_9

Functions and Closures

As you might know, "functions as a first-class feature" is the basis of functional programming. *First-class feature* means that a function can be used anywhere a value could be used.

For example, in JavaScript, you can assign a function to a variable and call it:

```
1    var func = function(x) { return x + 1; }
2    var three = func(2); //3
```

Although Groovy doesn't have first-class functions, it has something very similar: closures. As you have learned, a closure is simply a block of code wrapped in curly brackets with parameters defined to the left of the -> (arrow). For example:

```
1    def  closr = {x -> x + 1}
2    println( closr(2) ); //3
```

If a closure has one argument, it can be referenced as it in Groovy. For example:

```
1    def  closr = {it + 1}
```

Q Tip   In Groovy, the `return` keyword can be omitted if the returned value is the last expression.

Using Closures

As discussed previously, when a closure is the last parameter to a method, it can go outside of the parentheses, and if it is the only parameter, parentheses can be omitted completely. For example, the following defines a method that takes a list and a closure for filtering items:

```
1   def find(list, tester) {
2       for (item in list)
3           if (tester(item)) return item
4   }
```

This method returns the first item in the list for which the closure returns true. Here's an example of calling the method with a simple closure:

```
1   find([1,2]) { it > 1 }
```

Map/Filter/And So On

Once you have mastered functions, you quickly realize you need a way to perform operations on collections (or sequences or streams) of data.

Since these are common operations, people invented *sequence operations*, such as map, filter, reduce, etc.

For this section, we will be using a list of Person objects for all the operations (see Figures 9-1 through 9-5) defined as follows:

```
class Person {
    String name
    int age
    String toString() { name }
}
def persons = [new Person(name:'Bob',age:20),
        new Person(name:'Tom',age:15)]
```

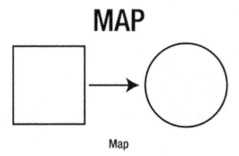

Map

Figure 9-1. *Map (collect): Translates or changes input elements into something else*

```
1    def names = persons.collect { person -> person.name }
// Result: ['Bob', 'Tom']
```

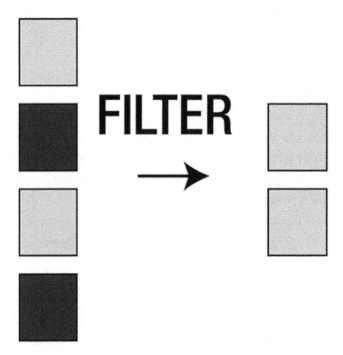

Filter

Figure 9-2. *Filter (findAll): Gives you a sub-set of elements (what returns true from some predicate function)*

```
1    def adults = persons.findAll { person -> person.age >= 18 }
// Result: [Bob]
```

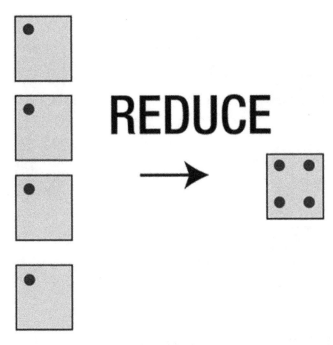

Reduce

Figure 9-3. *Reduce (inject): Performs a reduction (returning one result, such as a sum) on the elements*

```
1    def totalAge = persons.inject(0) {total, p -> return
     total+p.age } //Result: 35
```

For this, we use the `inject` method, which loops through the values and returns a single value (equivalent of `foldRight` in Scala). The `startValue` (0 in this case) is the initial value given to `total`. For each element of the list, we add the person's age.

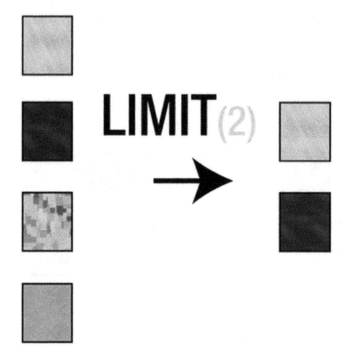

Limit

Figure 9-4. *Limit ([0..n-1]): Gives you only the first N elements*

```
1  def a = [3,2,1]
2  def firstTwo = a[0..1] // Result: [3,2]
```

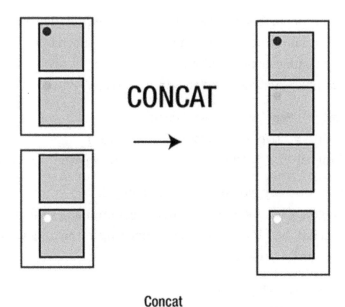

Concat

Figure 9-5. *Concat (+): Combines two different collections of elements*

```
1  def a = [1,2,3]
2  def b = [4,5]
3  a+b
4  // Result: [1, 2, 3, 4, 5]
```

Immutability

Immutability and FP go together like peanut butter and jelly. Although it's not necessary, they go together nicely.

In purely functional languages, the idea is that each function has no effect outside itself—that is, no side effects. This means that every time you call a function, it returns the same value given the same inputs.

To accommodate this behavior, there are *immutable* data structures. An immutable data structure cannot be directly changed but returns a new data structure with every operation.

For example, Scala's default Map is immutable:

```
1  val map = Map("Smaug" -> "deadly")
2  val map2 = map + ("Norbert" -> "cute")
3  println(map2) // Map(Smaug -> deadly, Norbert -> cute)
```

So in this code, map would remain unchanged.

Each language has a keyword for defining immutable variables (values). Java has the final keyword for declaring immutable variables, which Groovy also respects.

```
1  public class Centaur {
2      final String name
3      public Centaur(name) {this.name=name}
4  }
5  Centaur c = new Centaur("Bane");
6  println(c.name) // Bane
7  c.name = "Firenze" //groovy.lang.ReadOnlyPropertyException...
```

In addition to the final keyword, Groovy includes the @Immutable annotation[2] for declaring a whole class immutable. It also adds a default constructor (same as @TupleConstructor which adds a parameter for initializing each field), hashCode, equals, and toString methods. For example (in Groovy):

```
1  import groovy.transform.Immutable
2  @Immutable
3  public class Dragon {
4      String name
```

---

[2]http://docs.groovy-lang.org/latest/html/documentation/#xform-Immutable

```
5        int scales
6    }
7    Dragon smaug = new  Dragon('Smaug', 499)
8    println smaug
9    // Output: Dragon(Smaug, 499)
```

This works for simple references and primitives, such as numbers and strings, but for things like lists and maps, it's more complicated. For these cases, open source immutable libraries have been developed—for example, Guava[3] for Java and Groovy. To use existing immutable classes, you can set them using the knownImmutableClasses attribute. For example (after adding Guava to your Gradle build dependencies using compile "com.google.guava:guava:27.0-jre" or similar), see the following:

```
1    import com.google.common.collect.ImmutableList
2    import groovy.transform.CompileStatic
3    import groovy.transform.Immutable
4    /** Groovy Guava List: has internal ImmutableList. */
5    @Immutable(knownImmutableClasses = [ImmutableList])
6    @CompileStatic
7    class GroovyGuavaList<T> {
8        final ImmutableList<T> list
9    }
```

✏️ **Exercise**   Using the skills learned from previous chapters, create your own GroovyGuavaList class that overrides operators and is backed by an ImmutableList from Guava. Then use a Category or Extension module to add a method to java.util.List named toGList() that converts the list to a GroovyGuavaList.

---

[3]https://github.com/google/guava

85

Groovy Fluent GDK

In Groovy, findAll and other methods are available on every object, but they are especially useful for lists, sets, and ranges. In addition to findAll, collect, and inject, the following method names are used in Groovy:

- each—Iterates through the values using the given closure

- eachWithIndex—Iterates through with two parameters: a value and an index

- find—Finds the first element that matches a closure

- findIndexOf—Finds the first element that matches a closure and returns its index

For example, collect makes it very simple to perform an operation on a list of values, collecting the results into a new list:

```
1  def  list = ['foo','bar']
2  def newList = []
3  list.collect( newList ) { it.substring(1) }
4  println newList // [oo, ar]
```

For another example, assuming dragons is a list of dragon objects using the definition previously given:

```
1  def dragons = [new Dragon('Smaug', 499),
   new Dragon('Norbert', 488)]
2  String longestName = dragons.
3      findAll { it.name != null }.
4      collect { it.name }.
5      inject("") { n1, n2 -> n1.length() > n2.length() ? n1 : n2 }
```

The result should be Norbert. This code finds all non-null names, collects the names, and then reduces the list of names to the longest one.

Q Tip   Remember that **it** in Groovy can be used to reference a single argument of a closure.

✎ Exercise   Using the previous code as a starting point, find the dragon with the most scales.

Groovy Curry

The curry method allows you to predefine values for parameters of a closure. It takes any number of arguments and replaces parameters from left to right as you might expect. For example, given a concat closure, you could create a burn closure and an inate closure easily as follows:

```
1   def concat = { x, y -> return x + y }
2   // closure
3   def burn = concat.curry("burn")
4   def inate = concat.curry("inate")
```

Since you're only providing the first parameter, these closures are prepending their given text: burn prepends "burn" and inate prepends "inate". For example:

```
1   burn(" wood") // == burn wood
```

You could then use another closure called composition to apply the two functions to one input.

```
1   def composition = { f, g, x -> return f(g(x)) }
2   def burninate = composition.curry(burn, inate)
3   def trogdor = burninate(' all the people')
4   println "Trogdor: ${trogdor}"
5   // Trogdor: burninate all the people
```

Functional composition is an important idea in functional programming. It allows you compose functions together to create complex algorithms out of simple building blocks.

Method Handles

Method handles allow you to refer to actual methods much like they are closures. They are similar to Java method references except they give you additional functionality inherent to closures, such as the curry method described previously. This is useful when you want to use existing methods instead of closures, or you just want an alternative syntax for closures. For example, given a method:

```
1    def breathFire(name) { println "Burninating $name!" }
```

You could later on do the following to use a method handle to the method (within the same class that defined breathFire):

```
1    ['the country side', 'all the people'].each(this.&breathFire)
```

This would pass the breathFire method to the each method as a closure, causing the following to be printed:

```
1    Burninating the country side!
2    Burninating all the people!
```

✏️ **Exercise**   Create a method with multiple parameters and attempt to call it using a method handle. Does it work as expected?

Tail Recursion

In Groovy 1.8, the trampoline method was introduced for a closure to use the tail recursion optimization. This allows closure invocations to be invoked sequentially instead of stacked to avoid a StackOverFlowError and improve performance.

Starting in Groovy 2.3, you can use trampoline for recursive methods, but the @TailRecursive AST transformation is even simpler to use. Simply annotate a tail-recursive method with @TailRecursive and Groovy does the rest. For example:

```
1  import   groovy.transform.*
2  @TailRecursive
3  long  totalPopulation(list, total = 0) {
4    if (list.size() == 0)
5      total
6    else
7      totalPopulation(list.tail(), total + list.first().
         population)
8  }
```

ⓘ Info   On a Groovy list, the tail method returns the list without the first element and first returns just the first element.

This would take a list of objects with a population property and get the sum of them. For example, let's make a City class, use a range to create a bunch of them, and then use our totalPopulation method:

```
1  @Canonical class City {int population}
2  def cities = (10..1000).collect{new City(it)}
3  totalPopulation(cities)
4  // 500455
```

This demonstrates how tail recursion can be used in a functional style as an alternative to iteration.

ⓘ Info   Tail recursion goes well with immutability because no direct modification of variables is necessary in tail recursion.

Summary

In this chapter, you learned about the following:

- Functions as a first-class feature as closures

- Map/filter/reduce as `collect/findAll/inject`

- Immutability and how it relates to FP

- Various features that support FP in Groovy

- Method handles in Groovy

- Tail recursion optimization

CHAPTER 10

Groovy GPars

GPars[1] is an open source project to bring many concurrency abstractions to Java and/or Groovy. It was bundled in Groovy for a short time and then later pulled out.

It includes parallel map/reduce, Actors, Dataflow, and many other concurrency models. Although any concurrency library made for Java, such as RxJava, Project Reactor, or Akka, can be used with Groovy, GPars was made with Groovy specifically in mind.

Getting Started

To get started you first need to include GPars in your project. For example, in a Gradle build file, add the following to your dependencies block:

```
compile "org.codehaus.gpars:gpars:1.2.1"
```

For a maven build, add the following to your dependencies:

```
<dependency>
    <groupId>org.codehaus.gpars</groupId>
    <artifactId>gpars</artifactId>
    <version>1.2.1</version>
</dependency>
```

---

[1]http://gpars.org/

© Adam L. Davis 2019
A. L. Davis, *Learning Groovy 3*, https://doi.org/10.1007/978-1-4842-5058-7_10

Parallel Map Reduce

In this section we will use a list of students with graduation years and GPAs.

```
class Student { int graduationYear; double gpa; }
// create a list of students
Collection<Student> students = new ArrayList<>()
```

You perform parallel map/reduce with the GPars library in the following way:

```
1   GParsPool.withPool {
2       // a map-reduce functional style
3       def bestGpa = students.parallel
4           .filter{ s -> s.graduationYear==Student.THIS_YEAR }
5           .map{ s -> s.gpa }
6           .max()
7   }
```

The static method `GParsPool.withPool` takes in a closure and augments any Collection with several methods (using Groovy's Category mechanism). The `parallel` method actually creates a `ParallelArray` (JSR-166[2]) from the given Collection and uses it with a thin wrapper around it.[3]

Actors

The *Actor design pattern* is a useful pattern for developing concurrent software. In this pattern, each Actor executes in its own thread and manipulates its own data. The data cannot be manipulated by any other

---

[2]https://jcp.org/en/jsr/detail?id=166
[3]http://gpars.org/1.2.1/guide/guide/dataParallelism.
html#dataParallelism_map-reduce

thread. Messages are passed (internally by GPars) between the Actors to cause them to change the data. You can also make stateless Actors.

When data can be changed by only one thread at a time, it's called *thread-safe*.

```
0   @Grab("org.codehaus.gpars:gpars:1.2.1")
1   import groovyx.gpars.actor.Actor
2   import groovyx.gpars.actor.DefaultActor
3
4   class Dragon extends DefaultActor {
5       int age
6
7       void afterStart() {
8           age = new Random().nextInt(1000) + 1
9       }
11      void act() {
12          loop {
13              react { int num ->
14                  if (num > age)
15                  reply 'too old'
16                  else if (num < age)
17                  reply 'too young'
18                  else {
19                      reply 'you guessed right!'
20                      terminate()
21                  }
22              }
23          }
24      }
25  }
```

```
26    // Guesses the age of the Dragon
27    class Guesser extends DefaultActor {
28        String name
29        Actor server
30        int myNum
31
32        void act() {
33            loop {
34                myNum = new Random().nextInt(1000) + 1
35                server.send myNum
36                react {
37                    switch (it) {
38                        case 'too old': println "$name: $myNum was
                            too old"; break
39                        case 'too young': println "$name: $myNum was
                            too young"; break
40                        default: println "$name: I won $myNum";
                            terminate(); break
41                    }
42                }
43            }
44        }
45    }
46
47    def master = new Dragon().start()
48    def player = new Guesser(name: 'Guesser', server: master).
    start()
49
50    //this forces main thread to live until both actors stop
51    [master, player]*.join()
```

Here the `Dragon` class starts with some random age between 1 and 1000. It then reacts to a given number, replying if the number is too big, too small, or the same as its age. The `Guesser` class loops, generating a random guess each time through the loop and sending it to the `Dragon` (referred to as `server`). The `Guesser` then reacts to the message from the `Dragon` and terminates when the correct age was guessed.

The output will be something like the following:

```
Guesser: 236 was too young
... many other guesses
Guesser: 819 was too old
Guesser: I won 527
```

More GPars

For more information on other parts of GPars, such as Agents (which are much like Actors with functions as messages), Dataflow (an alternative concurrency model with deterministic behavior), and STM (Software Transactional Memory, which gives developers transactional syntax for dealing with in-memory state), please see GPars' excellent guide online.[4]

---

[4]www.gpars.org/guide/

PART III

The Groovy Ecosystem

There are many different frameworks and libraries built on top of Groovy (or support it as an option) that make up the Groovy ecosystem.

CHAPTER 11

Groovy Awesomeness

This short chapter introduces various useful frameworks within the Groovy ecosystem. Some of these will be described more fully in later chapters.

Web and UI Frameworks

The following are web and user interface frameworks that are built on top of Groovy or where Groovy is supported.

Grails[1]

A web framework inspired by Ruby on Rails. It has at least 800 plugins and uses convention over configuration approach.

Micronaut[2]

A newer framework for building microservices, serverless applications, or command-line applications with a small memory footprint and fast start-up speed with compile-time annotation processing. Built by the same group behind Grails.

---

[1]https://grails.org/
[2]https://micronaut.io/

© Adam L. Davis 2019
A. L. Davis, *Learning Groovy 3*, https://doi.org/10.1007/978-1-4842-5058-7_11

Griffon[3]

A framework for building Swing UIs. It has a command-line interface very similar to Grails. For example, `create-app cool -archetype=jumpstart`.

Vert.x[4]

A framework for asynchronous application development. Not strictly a Groovy project, but you can use it. It's currently an Eclipse Foundation project.[5]

Ratpack[6]

A toolkit for asynchronous web applications on the JVM and web services (microservices). Built on top of Netty.

Cloud Computing Frameworks

Cloud computing has become a mainstream necessity in today's programming world. Here are two useful Groovy frameworks for two popular cloud platforms.

Gaelyk[7]

An abstraction over GAE (Google App Engine); it has an emerging plugin system.

---

[3]http://new.griffon-framework.org/

[4]http://vertx.io/

[5]https://groups.google.com/forum/?fromgroups=#!topic/vertx/306NCDQQdUU

[6]www.ratpack.io/

[7]http://gaelyk.appspot.com/

Caelyf[8]

Apache 2-licensed framework for CloudFoundry. It's similar to gaelyk.

Build Frameworks

No project is complete without a build framework. Gradle has become more and more popular in the last few years especially for building Java projects. It's also the default build framework for Android and Grails projects.

Gradle[9]

It uses a Groovy-based DSL for building projects (it has added a Kotlin-based DSL as well) and uses `build.gradle` as the main build file. It has a very large plugin ecosystem and can be used to build any type of application.

Gant[10]

Like Ant in Groovy. It's now in maintenance mode. It was used by Grails and Griffon in the past.

Testing Frameworks/Code Analysis

Testing is extremely important for any project, and code analysis is sometimes useful for large projects. We will cover one of these frameworks, called Spock, in a later chapter.

---

[8]https://github.com/caelyf/caelyf
[9]www.gradle.org/
[10]https://gant.github.io/

Spock[11]

A very slick Groovy-based DSL testing framework that has been around for many years. It has the ability to use data tables for test input, built-in ability to mock classes and interfaces, and many other features.

Codenarc[12]

Static code analysis for Groovy and has been around since 2009. It has plugins for Grails and Griffon.

Concurrency

As described earlier, concurrency is extremely important for efficient applications to take complete advantage of the hardware.

GPars[13]

A multi-threading framework for Groovy. It has a fork/join abstraction, Actors, Dataflow, STM, and more.

RxGroovy[14]

This is a Groovy adapter to RxJava, a library for composing asynchronous and event-based programs using observable sequences for the JVM. However, it's no longer necessary—you can just use the RxJava library directly.

---

[11]http://spockframework.org
[12]http://codenarc.sourceforge.net/
[13]www.gpars.org/
[14]https://github.com/ReactiveX/RxGroovy

Others

These are other tools created by the community for managing your installed programming frameworks and tools and for creating new projects.

SDKMAN[15]

Originally called Groovy enVironment Manager (GVM). It's now called SDKMAN (Software Development Kit Manager) and is very cool. It allows you to manage multiple versions of several Groovy and non-Groovy SDKs, including Groovy itself.

Lazybones[16]

A simple project creation tool that uses packaged project templates. This can be installed using sdkman. It creates the basic files necessary to start various types of projects. For example, it has a Ratpack template.

GrooCSS[17]

A Groovy-based DSL for creating CSS. It's much like LESS but with everything Groovy has to offer available.

---

[15]https://sdkman.io/

[16]https://github.com/pledbrook/lazybones

[17]www.groocss.org/

CHAPTER 12

Gradle

Gradle is a build tool for the JVM with a Groovy-based DSL for building projects. The Gradle web site describes it as follows:

> Gradle combines the power and flexibility of Ant with the dependency management and conventions of Maven into a more effective way to build. Powered by a Groovy DSL and packed with innovation, Gradle provides a declarative way to describe all kinds of builds through sensible defaults.
>
> —gradle.org (2015)[1]

Projects and Tasks

Each Gradle build is composed of one or more projects and each project is composed of tasks. The core of the Gradle build is the `build.gradle` file (which is called the *build script*).

To try it out, go to `www.gradle.org` and install Gradle. Then create your own `build.gradle` file.

---

[1]`www.gradle.org/`

© Adam L. Davis 2019
A. L. Davis, *Learning Groovy 3*, https://doi.org/10.1007/978-1-4842-5058-7_12

Tasks can be defined by writing `task` and then a task name followed by a closure. Use the `doLast` method with a closure to execute any arbitrary code. For example:

```
1    task upper { doLast {
2            String someString = 'test'
3            println "Original: $someString"
4            println "Uppercase: " + someString.toUpperCase()
5    }}
```

Tasks can contain any Groovy code.

Much like in Ant, a task can depend on other tasks, which means they need to be run before the task. You simply call `dependsOn` with any number of task names as the arguments. For example:

```
1    task buildApp {
2            dependsOn clean, installApp, processAssets
3    }
```

You can also use the following alternative syntax:

```
1    task buildApp(dependsOn: [clean, installApp, processAssets])
```

⚷ Tip   Use the `doLast` method if your task contains the actual code you want the task to run. You are adding a closure to the task, not configuring the task. Otherwise, Gradle always runs the code in the first pass, not just when you invoke the task.

Once you've defined your tasks, you run them by invoking `gradle <task_name>` at the command line. There are some built-in tasks. For example, to list all available tasks, invoke the following:

```
1    gradle tasks
```

Plugins

Gradle core has very little built-in, but it has powerful plugins to allow it to be very flexible. A plugin can do one or more of the following:

- Add tasks to the project (e.g., compile and test).

- Pre-configure added tasks with useful defaults.

- Add dependency configurations to the project.

- Add new properties and methods to existing type via extensions.

We're going to concentrate on building Groovy-based projects, so we'll be using the Groovy plugin (however, Gradle is not limited to Groovy projects!):

```
1   apply plugin: 'groovy'
```

This plugin uses Maven's conventions. For example, it expects to find your main source code under src/main/groovy and your test source code under src/test/groovy.

Configuring a Task

Once you've added some plugins, you might want to configure some of the properties of a task for your purposes.

For example, you might want to specify a version of Gradle for the Gradle wrapper task:

```
1   task wrap(type: Wrapper) {
2       gradleVersion = '5.4.1'
3   }
```

The properties available depend on what task you are configuring. In the preceding case, we're configuring Gradle's Wrapper task to use Gradle version 5.4.1. Running this task would create a "gradlew" script file that can be run in place of gradle so that the same version of Gradle is run regardless of what is installed on the current machine. This is useful to make sure the build runs the same way every time.

Extra Configuration

To provide extra properties within your Gradle build file, use the ext method. You can define any arbitrary values within the closure, and they will be available throughout your project.

You can also apply properties from other Gradle build files. For example:

```
1  ext {
2      apply from: 'props/another.gradle'
3      myVersion = '1.2.3'
4  }
```

The properties defined within this closure can be used in your tasks or when defining your dependencies.

Dependencies

Every Java project tends to rely on many open source projects to be built. Gradle builds on Maven so you can easily include your dependencies using a simple DSL, like in the following example:

```
1  apply plugin: 'java'
2
3  sourceCompatibility = 1.11
4
```

```
5    repositories {
6            mavenLocal()
7            mavenCentral()
8    }
9
10      dependencies {
11              compile 'com.google.guava:guava:27.1-jre'
12              compile 'org.groocss:groocss:1.0-M2'

13              testCompile group: 'junit', name: 'junit',
                version: '5.+'
14              testCompile "org.mockito:mockito-core:2.28.2"
15      }
```

This build script uses sourceCompatibility to define the Java source code version of 1.11 (which is used during compilation). Next it tells Maven to use the local repository first (mavenLocal) and then Maven central.

In the dependencies block, this build script defines two dependencies for the compile scope and two for testCompile scope. Jars in the testCompile scope are only used by tests and won't be included in any final products.

The line for JUnit shows the more verbose style for defining dependencies. It also specifies, using +, that the version be 5.0 or greater.

You can also specify your own Maven repository by calling maven with a closure supplying the appropriate parameters (at least an URL). For example (in the repositories section):

```
1    maven {url "https://oss.sonatype.org/content/repositories/
     snapshots/" }
2    maven { url = "$nexus/content/groups/public"
3            credentials {
4                    username 'deployment'
5                    password deploymentPassword
6            }
7    }
```

The second example demonstrates using a secured Maven repository. It also demonstrates using the variables nexus and deploymentPassword which could (probably should) be stored in a gradle.properties file.

Gradle Properties

The gradle.properties file allows you to specify Gradle properties and other properties available to your build script. For example, you can specify JVM arguments and whether you want to use the Gradle daemon (which runs in the background and speeds up subsequent Gradle builds; this is the default):

```
1   org.gradle.daemon=true
2   org.gradle.jvmargs=-Xms128m -Xmx512m
```

You could also specify build-specific values that you don't want to keep in your versioning system (such as Nexus credentials). For example, you might add the following to your local gradle.properties file:

```
nexusUser=user
nexusPassword=changeme123
```

Now both nexusUser and nexusPassword would be available properties in your Gradle build file.

Multiproject Builds

A multiproject build can include any number of sub-projects that are built together. Each sub-project should be put in a directory under a single top directory, where the name of each directory is the name of the sub-project.

Separate builds in a multiproject build may depend on one another. You can express dependencies on any number of sub-projects using the following syntax:

```
1   dependencies {
2     compile project(':subproject1')
3     compile project(':subproject2')
4   }
```

The top-level build.gradle file of multiproject should look something like the following:

```
1   allprojects {
2     apply plugin: "groovy"
3   }
4   project(":subproject1") {
5     dependencies {}
6   }
7   project(":subproject2") {
8     dependencies {}
9   }
```

You can create sub-projects by creating a directory and putting a build.gradle file there. For example (on a Unix-like system):

```
mkdir subproject1
touch subproject1/build.gradle
mkdir subproject2
touch subproject2/build.gradle
```

Finally, you should create a file named settings.gradle that calls include with a list of sub-projects. For example, given the above sub-projects, use the following in settings.gradle:

```
include 'subproject1', 'subproject2'
```

111

File Operations

Since Gradle evaluates tasks before actually executing them, you should generally not use `java.util.File` directly for defining files or directories. Instead, Gradle provides a number of built-in methods and tasks. For example, you should use the `file` method for single files or directories and the `files` method to define a collection of files or directories.

```
1   outputDir = file("libs/x86")
```

There's also a `fileTree` method for recursively listing a directory of files. For example, you can depend on all files under the `lib` directory in the following way:

```
1   dependencies {
2           compile fileTree('lib')
3   }
```

To copy files from one place to another, use the Copy task. Here's a good example:

```
1   task copyImages(type: Copy) {
2           from 'assets'
3           into 'build/images'
4           include '**/*.jpg'
5           exclude '**/*test*'
6   }
```

This task would copy all images that end with `.jpg` from the `assets` directory into the `build/images` directory, excluding any files containing the word `test`.

Exploring

Remember you can also easily list properties of an object in Groovy using .properties. This can help you explore available Gradle properties at runtime. For example:

```
1   task testIt {
2           doLast { println sourceSets.main.properties }
3   }
```

Completely Groovy

Remember that all of Groovy's goodness is available in Gradle. For example, the following one-liner sets the encoding option to UTF-8 for two tasks using the "star-dot" notation (this is useful when your code contains non-ASCII characters):

```
1   [compileJava, compileTestJava]*.options*.encoding = 'UTF-8'
```

✏ **Exercise**   Explore Gradle by making your own build.gradle and trying out everything in this chapter.

Summary

This chapter taught you the following about Gradle:

- How to create tasks

- How to use plugins

- How to specify dependencies

- What gradle.properties is all about

- How to create multiproject builds

- Using built-in methods for file operations

ℹ **Online Documentation**   Gradle has a huge online user guide available at www.gradle.org.[2]

---

[2]www.gradle.org/docs/current/userguide/userguide.html

CHAPTER 13

Grails

Grails is a web framework for Groovy that follows the example of *Ruby on Rails* to be an opinionated web framework with a command-line tool that gets things done really fast. Grails uses convention over configuration to reduce configuration overhead.

Grails lives firmly in the Java ecosystem and is built on top of technologies like Spring and Hibernate. Grails also includes (optionally) an object relational mapping (ORM) framework called *GORM* and has a large collection of plugins.

Different versions of Grails can be very different, so you need to take care when upgrading your Grails application, especially with major versions (2.5 to 3.0, for example).

This chapter contains a quick overview of how Grails (3.3) works and then includes a short history of Grails.

Quick Overview of Grails

After installing Grails,[1] you can create an app by running the following on the command-line (replace TEST with the name of the directory you want to use):

```
1    $ grails create-app TEST
```

---

[1]This overview is based on Grails 3.3.10 but should work with 4.0.

© Adam L. Davis 2019
A. L. Davis, *Learning Groovy 3*, https://doi.org/10.1007/978-1-4842-5058-7_13

By default this will create an application using the "web" profile (to get a list of available profiles, run `grails list-profiles`).

Then you can run commands like `create-domain-class` and `generate-all` to create your application as you go. Run `grails help` to see the full list of commands available.

Grails applications have a very specific project structure. The following is a simple breakdown of *most of* that structure:

- `grails-app`—The Grails-specific folder.

  - `assets`

    - `images`—Images used by your web application.

    - `javascripts`—Your JavaScript files go here.

    - `stylesheets`—CSS stylesheets.

  - `conf`—Configuration, such as an application.yml or application.properties file.

  - `controllers`—Controllers of the application and the `UrlMappings` class. Provides code for actions like list, save, show, and create.

  - `domain`—Domain model; classes representing your persistent data if you use GORM.

  - `i18n`—Message bundles which enable you to provide text in multiple different languages.

  - `init`—Includes `Application.groovy` and `BootStrap.groovy`.

  - `services`—Backend services where your backend or "business" logic goes.

  - `taglib`—You can very easily define your own tags for use in your GSP files here.

- views—Views of MVC; typically these are GSP files (HTML based).

- utils—Can contain utility classes.

- src—Any common code that doesn't fit anywhere else.

  - main/java—Java code

  - main/groovy—Groovy code

  - main/resources—Any non-code resources you want in the main classpath.

  - test/groovy—Groovy-based tests which can use JUnit or Spock.

  - integration-test/groovy—Includes Geb-based tests.

  - integration-test/resources—Includes GebConfig.groovy for configuring Geb.

To create a new domain (model) class, run a command like the following:

```
1   $ grails create-domain-class example.Post
```

It's a good idea to include a package for your domain classes (here the package is "example" and the class is named Post).

A domain class in Grails also defines its mapping to the database. For example, here's a domain class representing a blog post (assuming User and Comment were already created):

```
1   class Post {
2       String text
3       int rating
4       Date created = new Date()
5       User createdBy
6
```

```
7        static hasMany = [comments: Comment]
8
9        static constraints = {
10            text(size:10..5000)
11        }
12    }
```

The static hasMany field is a map that represents one-to-many relationships in your database. GORM uses Hibernate in the background to create tables for all of your domain classes and relationships. Every table gets an id field for the primary key by default.

To have Grails automatically create your controller and views, run the following:

```
1    $ grails generate-all example.Post
```

⚠️ **Warning**   Grails will ask if you want to overwrite existing files if they exist. Be careful when using this command.

When you want to run your application directly to try it out, you can simply run the following:

```
1    $ grails run-app
```

If you want to deploy to an application container (e.g., Tomcat), you can create a war file by running the following:

```
1    $ grails war
```

Configuration

Since Grails 3+ is built on Spring Boot, configuration works in a similar way using the grails-app/conf/application.yml file by default.

Toward the bottom of this file, you'll see the default configuration uses an in-memory h2 database for development and test and a file-based h2 database for production. They are configured as follows (this is where you would change the configuration to change your database):

```
development:
    dataSource:
            dbCreate: create-drop
            url: jdbc:h2:mem:devDb;MVCC=TRUE;LOCK_TIMEOUT=10000;
DB_CLOSE_ON_EXIT=FALSE
test:
    dataSource:
            dbCreate: update
            url: jdbc:h2:mem:testDb;MVCC=TRUE;LOCK_TIMEOUT=10000;
DB_CLOSE_ON_EXIT=FALSE
production:
    dataSource:
            dbCreate: none
            url: jdbc:h2:./prodDb;MVCC=TRUE;LOCK_TIMEOUT=10000;
DB_CLOSE_ON_EXIT=FALSE
            properties:
                jmxEnabled: true
                initialSize: 5
...(cut for brevity)
```

Plugins

The Grails ecosystem includes over 100 plugins. To list all of the plugins, simply execute this command:

```
1   $ grails list-plugins
```

When you've picked a plugin you want to use, execute the following command to see the available versions and how to include it in your build dependencies (with the plugin name):

```
1   $ grails plugin-info [NAME]
```

This will show you the appropriate code to add to your build.gradle file for adding the plugin to your project. For example, let's look at the "geb" plugin (Geb is a web testing framework). Here is the output:

```
$ grails plugin-info geb
| Plugin Info: geb
| Latest Version: 2.0.0
| All Versions: 1.0.2,1.1.1,1.1.2,1.1.3,1.1.4,1.1.5,2.0.0.RC1,2.0.0
| Title: Geb Plugin

Plugin that adds Geb functional testing code generation features.

* License: APACHE
* Documentation: http://grails.org/plugin/geb
* Issue Tracker: http://github.com/grails3-plugins/geb/issues
* Source: http://github.com/grails3-plugins/geb
* Definition:

dependencies {
        compile "org.grails.plugins:geb:2.0.0"
}
```

GSP and Taglibs

Grails uses GSP by default for generating views in a web application. Take a look at the grails-app/views directory. You should see an index.gsp file which generates the landing page for your application. If you generated the example.Post views as described earlier you will also see some GSP files under a "post" directory. These generate the pages for showing, listing, creating, and editing Posts.

GSP is based on HTML with the addition of its own built-in tag libraries (starting with the g: prefix). You can add you own tag library by adding a class ending with TagLib to the grails-app/taglib directory. For example, add a file named SimpleTagLib.groovy to the taglib directory with the following code (which would format dates with a given format):

```
class SimpleTagLib {
    static namespace = "my" // changes from g: namespace to my:
    def dateFormat = { attrs, body ->
      out << new
    java.text.SimpleDateFormat(attrs.format).format(attrs.date)
    }
}
```

This would now allow you to use the following tag in your gsp files:

```
<my:dateFormat format="dd-MM-yyyy" date="${new Date()}" />
```

Serving JSON or XML

Groovy includes some built-in support for JSON (JavaScript Object Notation) encoding and decoding, including the JsonSlurper. Grails also includes converters for easily converting objects to XML or JSON or vice

121

versa. For example, see the following PostController with methods for rendering Posts as JSON and XML:

```
1    import grails.converters.JSON
2    import grails.converters.XML
3
4    class PostController {
5            def getPosts() {
6                    render Post.list() as JSON
7            }
8            def getPostsXML() {
9                    render Post.list() as XML
10           }
11   }
```

For web services that service multiple formats, you can use the built-in withFormat in Grails. So the above code could be reduced to the following:

```
1    def getPosts() {
2            withFormat {
3                    json { render list as JSON }
4                    xml { render list as XML }
5            }
6    }
```

Then Grails would decide which format to use based on numerous inputs, the simplest being the extension of the URL, such as .json, or the request's Accept header.

For *using* web services in Grails, you could use the http-builder-helper plugin[2] or you could use the built-in HTTP client from Micronaut (included in Grails 4).

---

[2]http://plugins.grails.org/plugin/grails/http-builder-helper

UrlMappings

By default, Grails reads the UrlMappings class to determine how to
route incoming requests to your web application. It consists of a static
value named "mappings" that uses a DSL to describe the routing of the
application. The default UrlMappings for a new project looks like the
following:

```
class UrlMappings {
    static mappings = {
        "/$controller/$action?/$id?(.$format)?"{
            constraints {
                // apply constraints here
            }
        }
        "/"(view:"/index")
        "500"(view:'/error')
        "404"(view:'/notFound')
    }
}
```

The variables controller, action, id, and format within the first
GString take on a special meaning in this context. Using them in this
way will match any value given and set the corresponding variable to it.
For example, the path **/post/show/123** would initiate the "show" action
on the PostController with a parameter ID of 123. You can modify the
mappings to create custom paths. For example, you could create a custom
route to create a new post like this: "/new/post/" (controller: "post",
action: "create").

The first path matched is what route Grails will use.

Short History of Grails

What follows is a brief history of the features added to Grails starting with version 2.0.

Grails 2.0

There were the following improvements in Grails 2.0:

- Better error page that shows code what caused the problem.

- H2 database console in development mode (at the URI `/dbconsole`).

- Grails 2.0 supports Groovy 1.8.

- Runtime reloading for typed services, domain classes, `src/groovy`, and `src/java`.

- Run any command with `-reloading` to dynamically reload it.

- Binary plugins (jars).

- Better scaffolding that's HTML 5 compliant (mobile/tablet ready).

- PageRenderer and LinkGenerator API for services.

- Servlet 3.0 async API supported; events plugin; platform core.

- Resources plugin integrated into core.

- Plugins for GZIP, cache, bundling (`install-plugin` `cached-resources`, `zipped-resources`).

- New tags: `img`, `external`, and `javascript`.

- The jQuery plugin is now the default JavaScript library installed in a Grails application.

- A new `date` method has been added to the `params` object to allow easy, null-safe parsing of dates: `def val = params.date('myDate', 'dd-MM-yyyy')`.

Various GORM improvements include:

- Support for `DetachedCriteria` and new `findOrCreate` and `findOrSave` methods.

- GORM supports MongoDB,[3] riak,[4] Cassandra,[5] neo4j,[6] redis,[7] and Amazon SimpleDB.[8]

- New compile-time checked query DSL ("where" method which takes a Closure parameter) which includes: `avg`, `sum`, `subqueries`, `.size()`, and so on.

- Multiple scoped data sources.

- Added database migration plugin for updating production databases.

Grails 2.1

- Grails' Maven support has been improved in a number of significant ways. For example, it is now possible to specify plugins within your `pom.xml` file.

- The `grails` command now supports a `-debug` option which will start the remote debug agent.

---

[3]`www.mongodb.org/`
[4]`https://riak.com/`
[5]`http://cassandra.apache.org/`
[6]`https://neo4j.org/`
[7]`https://redis.io/`
[8]`https://aws.amazon.com/simpledb/`

- Installs the cache plugin by default.

- In Grails 2.1.1, domain classes now have static methods named `first` and `last` that retrieve the first and last instances from the datastore.

Grails 2.2

- Grails 2.2 supports Groovy 2.

- Adds new functionality to criteria queries to provide access to Hibernate's SQL projection API.

- Supports forked JVM execution of the Tomcat container in development mode.

- Includes improved support for managing naming conflicts between artifacts provided by an application and its plugins.

Grails 2.3

- Improved dependency management using the same library used by Maven (Aether) by default.

- Includes a new data binding mechanism that's more flexible and easier to maintain than the data binder used in previous versions.

- All major commands can now be forked into a separate JVM, thus isolating the build path from the runtime and test paths.

- Grails' REST support has been significantly improved.

- Grails' scaffolding feature has been split into a separate plugin (includes support for generating REST controllers, async controllers, and Spock unit tests).

- Includes new asynchronous programming APIs that allow for asynchronous processing of requests and integrates seamlessly with GORM.

- Controllers may now be defined in a namespace that allows for multiple controllers to be defined with the same name in different packages.

Grails 2.4

- Grails 2.4 comes with Groovy 2.3.

- Uses Hibernate 4.3.5 by default. (Hibernate 3 is still available as an optional install.)

- The Asset-Pipeline replaces Resources to serve static assets.

- Now has great support for static type checking and static compilation. The `GrailsCompileStatic` annotation (from the `grails.compiler` package) behaves much like the `groovy.transform.Compi` annotation and provides special handling for Grails.

Grails 2.5

- Upgraded to Groovy 2.4

- Spring upgrading to 4.1

- Other various upgrades

Grails 3.1.x

Grails 3 represents a huge refactoring of Grails. The public API is now located in the `grails` package and everything has been redone to use Traits. Each new project also features an `Application` class with a traditional static void main.

Grails 3 comes with Groovy 2.4, Spring 4.1, and Spring Boot 1.2, and the build system uses Gradle (instead of the previously used Gant system).

Among other changes, the use of filters has been deprecated and should be replaced with interceptors. To create a new interceptor, use the following command:

```
1    grails create-interceptor MyInterceptor
```

An interceptor contains the following methods:

```
1    boolean before() { true }
2    boolean after() { true }
3    void afterView() {}
```

- The `before` method is executed before a matched action. The return value determines whether the action should execute, allowing you to cancel the action.

- The `after` method is executed after the action executes but prior to view rendering. Its return value determines whether the view rendering should execute.

- The `afterView` method is executed after view rendering completes.

Grails 3 supports built-in support for Spock/Geb functional tests using the `create-functional-test` command.

Grails 4

Grails 4 included updates to the versions of the underlying libraries like Spring Boot as well as integration of Micronaut into the core. The following are the minimum library versions supported in Grails 4.0:

- Spring 5.1

- Spring Boot 2.1

- Java 8

- Hibernate 5.4

- Groovy 2.5

Testing

Grails supports unit testing with a mixin approach. It inludes the following annotations:

- `@TestFor(X)`—Specifies the class under test

- `@Mock(Y)`—Creates a mock for the given class

For tests, GORM provides an in-memory mock database that uses `ConcurrentHashMap`. You can create tests for tag libraries, command objects, URL-Mappings, XML and JSON, and so on.

Cache Plugin

The cache plugin can be used to cache content to enhance the performance of web applications.

- You can add the @Cacheable annotation on service or controller methods.

- Cache tags include cache:block and cache:render.

- Related plugins include cache-ehcache, cache-guava, and cache-headers.

 Only an Overview   This has been a brief overview of Grails. Many books have been written about Grails and how to use it. For more information on using Grails, visit https://grails.org.[9]

✏ **Exercise**   Create your own Grails app.

---

[9]https://grails.org/

CHAPTER 14

Spock

Spock[1] is a testing framework for Java and Groovy applications that takes full advantage of Groovy and has object mocking integrated. The Spock web site[2] has this to say about Spock:

> Spock is a testing and specification framework for Java and Groovy applications. What makes it stand out from the crowd is its beautiful and highly expressive specification language. Thanks to its JUnit runner, Spock is compatible with most IDEs, build tools, and continuous integration servers. Spock is inspired from JUnit, RSpec, jMock, Mockito, Groovy, Scala, Vulcans, and other fascinating life forms.

Spock Basics

The basic structure of a test class in Spock is a class that extends `spock.lang.Specification` and has multiple test methods (which may have descriptive String names).

Spock processes the test code and allows you to use a simple Groovy syntax to specify tests.

---

[1]http://spockframework.org/
[2]https://code.google.com/p/spock/

© Adam L. Davis 2019
A. L. Davis, *Learning Groovy 3*, https://doi.org/10.1007/978-1-4842-5058-7_14

Each test is composed of labeled blocks of code with labels like when, then, and where. The best way to learn Spock is with examples.

To get started, first add Spock as a dependency to your project. For example, within a Gradle build file, put the following:

```
1   dependencies {
2     testCompile "org.spockframework:spock-core:1.3-groovy-2.5"
3   }
```

A Simple Test

Let's start by recreating a simple test:

```
1   def "toString yields the String representation"() {
2         def array = ['a', 'b', 'c'] as String[]
3         when:
4         def arrayWrapper = new ArrayWrapper<>(array)
5         then:
6         arrayWrapper.toString() == '[a, b, c]'
7   }
```

As shown, assertions are simply groovy conditional expressions. If the == expression returns false, the test will fail and Spock will give a detailed printout to explain why it failed.

In the absence of any when clause, you can use the expect clause instead of then; for example:

```
1   def "empty list size is zero"() {
2         expect: [].size() == 0
3   }
```

Mocking

Mocking interfaces is extremely easy in Spock.[3] Simply use the Mock method, as shown in the following example (where Subscriber is an interface):

```
1  class APublisher extends Specification {
2    def publisher = new Publisher()
3    def subscriber = Mock(Subscriber)
```

Now subscriber is a mocked object. You can implement methods simply using the overloaded >> operator as shown next. The following example throws an Exception whenever receive is called:

```
1  def "can cope with misbehaving subscribers"() {
2      subscriber.receive(_) >> { throw new Exception() }
3
4      when:
5      publisher.send("event")
6      publisher.send("event")
7
8      then:
9      2 * subscriber.receive("event")
10  }
```

The expected behavior can be described by using a number or range multiplied by (*) the method call, as shown here. This means to expect this method is called two times; otherwise the test will fail.

The underscore (_) is treated like a wildcard much like in Scala (here the _ is just a field that refers to an object defined by Spock).

---

[3]You can also mock classes, but it requires including the bytebuddy jar as a dependency: testRuntime "net.bytebuddy:byte-buddy:1.9.13"

Lists or Tables of Data

Much like how JUnit has DataPoints and Theories, Spock allows you to use lists or tables of data in tests.

For example:

```
1   def "subscribers receive published events at least once"(){
2       when: publisher.send(event)
3       then: (1.._) * subscriber.receive(event)
4       where: event << ["started", "paused", "stopped"]
5   }
```

The overloaded << operator is used to provide a list for the event variable. Although it is a list here, anything that is Iterable could be used. This has the effect of running the test for each value in the list.

Ranges   The range 1.._ here means "one or more" times. You can also use _..3, for example, to mean "three or fewer" times.

Tabular formatted data can be used as well. For example:

```
1    def "length of NASA mission names"() {
2        expect:
3        name.size() == length
4
5        where:
6        name        | length
7        "Mercury"   | 7
8        "Gemini"    | 6
9        "Apollo"    | 6
10   }
```

In this case, the two columns (name and length) are used to substitute the corresponding variables in the expect block. Any number of columns can be used.

Expecting Exceptions

Use the "thrown" method in the then block to expect a thrown Exception.

```
1   def "peek on empty stack throws"() {
2       when: stack.peek()
3       then: thrown(EmptyStackException)
4   }
```

You can also capture the thrown Exception by simply assigning it to thrown(). For example:

```
1   def "peek on empty stack throws"() {
2       when: stack.peek()
3       then:
4       Exception e = thrown()
5       e.toString().contains("EmptyStackException")
6   }
```

Summary

As you can see, Spock makes tests more concise and easy to read, includes mocking built-in, and, most importantly, makes the intentions of the test clear.

CHAPTER 15

Ratpack

At its core, Ratpack[1] enables asynchronous, stateless HTTP applications. It is built on Netty, the event-driven networking engine. Unlike some web frameworks, there is no expectation that one thread handles one request. Instead, you are encouraged to handle blocking operations in a way that frees the current thread, thus allowing high performance.

Ratpack can be used to make responsive, RESTful microservices, although it's not a requirement.

Rest   stands for REpresentational State Transfer.[2] It was designed in a PhD dissertation and has gained much popularity as the new web service standard. At the most basic level in REST, each CRUD operation is mapped to an HTTP method (GET, POST, PUT, and so on).

Unlike Grails and other popular web frameworks, Ratpack aims not to be a framework, but instead a set of libraries. Although it's a lean set of libraries, Ratpack comes packed with support for JSON, websockets, SSE (server sent events), SSL, SQL, logging, Dropwizard Metrics, newrelic, health checks, hystrix, and more.

Ratpack uses Guice by default for DI (dependency injection).

---

[1]www.ratpack.io/
[2]www.ics.uci.edu/~fielding/pubs/dissertation/top.htm

© Adam L. Davis 2019
A. L. Davis, *Learning Groovy 3*, https://doi.org/10.1007/978-1-4842-5058-7_15

> **Q Tip**   Ratpack is written in Java (8) and you can write Ratpack applications in pure Java, but we are focusing on the Groovy side.

Script

In its simplest form, you can create a Ratpack application using only a Groovy script. For example, the following script would run a simple Ratpack application that always responds "Hello World!":

```
1   @Grab('io.ratpack:ratpack-groovy:1.6.1')
2
3   import static ratpack.groovy.Groovy.ratpack
4
5   ratpack {
6     handlers {
7       handler {
8         response.send "Hello World!"
9       }
10    }
11  }
```

Gradle

For production systems you should use a Gradle build. Ratpack has its own Gradle plugin that you can use, as follows (jcenter refers to the Maven central alternative, Bintray's JCenter):

```
1   buildscript {
2     repositories {
3       jcenter()
4     }
```

```
5    dependencies {
6        classpath 'io.ratpack:ratpack-gradle:1.6.1'
7    }
8  }
9
10   apply plugin: 'io.ratpack.ratpack-groovy'
11
12   repositories {
13     jcenter()
14   }
```

Using the `ratpack-gradle` plugin, you can run tasks, such as `distZip`, `distTar`, `installApp`, and `run`, which creates a ZIP distribution file, creates a TAR distribution file, installs the Ratpack application locally, and runs the application, respectively.

The `run` task is very useful for test driving your application. After invoking `gradle run`, you should see the following output:

```
1    [main] INFO ratpack.server.RatpackServer - Starting
     server...
2    [main] INFO ratpack.server.RatpackServer - Building
     registry...
3    [main] INFO ratpack.server.RatpackServer - Ratpack started
     (development)
4    for http://localhost:5050
```

Ratpack Layout

Unlike in Grails, you need to create these files and directories yourself (or use Lazybones).

- `build.gradle` (the Gradle build file)

- src

    - main/groovy—Where you put general Groovy classes

    - main/resources—Where you put static resources, such as Handlebars templates

    - ratpack—Contains Ratpack.groovy, which defines your Ratpack handlers and bindings and ratpack.properties

    - ratpack/public—Any public files like HTML, JavaScript, images, and CSS

    - ratpack/templates—Holds your Groovy markup templates (if you have any)

Handlers

Handlers are the basic building blocks for Ratpack. They form something like a pipeline or "chain of responsibility."[3] Multiple handlers can be called per request, but one must return a response. If none of your handlers is matched, a default handler returns a 404 status code.

```
1   import static ratpack.groovy.Groovy.ratpack
2
3   ratpack {
4     handlers {
5       all() { response.headers.add('x-custom', 'x'); next() }
6       get("foo") {
7           render "foo handler"
8       }
9       get(":key") {
10          def key = pathTokens.key
```

---

[3]www.oodesign.com/chain-of-responsibility-pattern.html

```
11              render "{\"key\": \"$key\"}"
12          }
13        files { dir "public" }
14      }
15    }
```

The first handler all() is used for every HTTP request and adds a custom header. It then calls next() so the next matching handler gets called. The next handler that matches a given HTTP request will be used to fulfill the request with a response.

The pathTokens map contains all parameters passed in the URL as specified in the matching path pattern, as in :key, by prefixing : to a variable name you specify. For example, if the preceding application is run, requesting /abc will get you the response {"key":"abc"}.

You can define a handler using a method corresponding to any one of the HTTP methods:

- Get

- Post

- Put

- Delete

- Patch

- Options

To accept multiple methods on the same path, you should use the path handler and byMethod with each method handler inside it. For example:

```
1  path("foo") {
2      byMethod {
3          post() { render 'post foo'}
```

```
4            put() { render 'put foo'}
5            delete() { render 'delete foo'}
6        }
7    }
```

Rendering

There are many ways to render a response. The "grooviest" ways are using the groovyMarkupTemplate or groovyTemplate methods.

For example, here's how to use the groovyMarkupTemplate:

```
1   import    ratpack.groovy.template.MarkupTemplateModule
2   import    static   ratpack.groovy.Groovy.
    groovyMarkupTemplate
3   import static ratpack.groovy.Groovy.ratpack
4   ratpack {
5     bindings {
6       module MarkupTemplateModule
7     }
8     handlers {
9       get(":key") {
10          def key = pathTokens.key
11          render groovyMarkupTemplate("index.gtpl",
            title: "$key")
12      }
13      files { dir "public" }
14    }
15  }
```

This allows you to use the Groovy markup language, and by default it looks in the ratpack/templates directory for markup files. For example, your index.gtpl might look like the following:

```
1    yieldUnescaped '<!DOCTYPE html>'
2    html {
3      head {
4        meta(charset:'utf-8')
5        title("Ratpack: $title")
6        meta(name: 'apple-mobile-web-app-title', content:
         'Ratpack')
7        meta(name: 'description', content: ")
8        meta(name: 'viewport', content: 'width=device-width,
         initial-scale=1')
9        link(href: '/images/favicon.ico', rel: 'shortcut icon')
10       }
11     body {
12       header {
13         h1 'Ratpack'
14         p 'Simple, lean & powerful HTTP apps'
15       }
16       section {
17         h2 title
18         p 'This is the main page for your Ratpack app.'
19       }
20     }
21   }
```

1. yieldUnescaped outputs the given String directly into the resulting HTML.

2. The Groovy markup language is a Groovy-based DSL to create HTML from Groovy code.

Groovy Text

If you prefer to use a plain old text document with embedded Groovy (much like a GString), you can use the TextTemplateModule:

```
1   import ratpack.groovy.template.TextTemplateModule
2   import static ratpack.groovy.Groovy.groovyTemplate
3   import static ratpack.groovy.Groovy.ratpack
4   ratpack {
5     bindings {
6       module TextTemplateModule
7     }
8     handlers {
9       get(":key") {
10          def  key = pathTokens.key
11          render groovyTemplate("index.html", title: "$key")
12        }
13      }
14   }
```

Then create a file named index.html in the src/main/resources/templates directory with the following content:

```
1   <html><h1>${model.title}</h1></html>
```

It supplies a model map to your template, which contains all of the parameters you supply.

Handlebars and Thymeleaf

Ratpack also supports Handlebars and Thymeleaf templates, two alternative methods of generating dynamic web pages. Since these are static resource, you should put these templates in the src/main/resources directory.

You will first need to include the appropriate Ratpack project in your Gradle build file:

```
1    runtime 'io.ratpack:ratpack-handlebars:1.6.1'
2    runtime 'io.ratpack:ratpack-thymeleaf3:1.6.1'
```

To use Handlebars (an alternative template format), include the HandlebarsModule and render Handlebar templates as follows:

```
1    import ratpack.handlebars.HandlebarsModule
2    import static   ratpack.handlebars.Template.
     handlebarsTemplate
3    import static ratpack.groovy.Groovy.ratpack
4    ratpack {
5      bindings {
6        module HandlebarsModule
7      }
8      handlers {
9        get("foo") {
10             render handlebarsTemplate('myTemplate.html',
               title: 'Handlebars')
11       }
12     }
13   }
```

Create a file named myTemplate.html.hbs (.hbs is the Handlebars suffix) in the src/main/resources/handlebars directory with Handlebar content. For example:

```
1    <span>{{title}}</span>
```

Thymeleaf works in a similar way:

```
1   import ratpack.thymeleaf.ThymeleafModule
2   import static   ratpack.thymeleaf.Template.
    thymeleafTemplate
3   import static ratpack.groovy.Groovy.ratpack
4   ratpack {
5     bindings {
6       module ThymeleafModule
7     }
8     handlers {
9       get("foo") {
10           render thymeleafTemplate('myTemplate',
             title: 'Thymeleaf')
11       }
12     }
13   }
```

The requested file should be named myTemplate.html and be located in the src/main/resources/thymeleaf directory of your project. Example content:

```
1   <span th:text=\"${title}\"/>
```

JSON

Integration with the Jackson JSON marshaling library provides the ability to work with JSON.

The ratpack.jackson.Jackson class provides most of the Jackson-related functionality. For example, to render JSON, you can use Jackson.json:

```
1   import static ratpack.jackson.Jackson.json
2   ratpack {
3     bindings {
4     }
5     handlers {
6       get("user") {
7         render json([user: 1])
8       }
9     }
10  }
```

The Jackson integration also includes a parser for converting JSON request bodies into objects. The Jackson.jsonNode() and Jackson.fromJson(Class) methods can be used to create parseable objects to be used with the parse() method.

For example, the following handler would parse a JSON String representing a Person object and render the Person's name:

```
1   post("personNames") {
2     render( parse(fromJson(Person.class)).map {it.name} )
3   }
```

Tip   Context.parse returns a ratpack.exec.Promise<T>. A Promise<T> is a commonly used pattern in concurrent programming that allows a simplified syntax. It implements methods such as map as shown previously.

Bindings

Bindings in Ratpack make objects available to the handlers. If you are familiar with Spring, Ratpack uses a *registry,* which is similar to the application context in Spring. It can also be thought of as a simple map from classtypes to instances. Ratpack-Groovy uses Guice by default, although other direct-injection frameworks, such as Spring, can be used (or none at all).

Instead of a formal plugin system, reusable functionality can be packaged as modules. You can create your own modules to properly decouple and organize your application into components. For example, you might want to create a MongoModule or a JdbcModule. Alternatively, you could break your application into services. Either way, the registry is where you put them.

Anything in the registry can be automatically used in a handler and gets wired in by classtype from the registry. Here's an example of bindings in action:

```
1   bindings {
2     bindInstance(MongoModule, new MongoModule())
3     bind(DragonService, DefaultDragonService)
4   }
5   handlers {
6     get('dragons') { DragonService dService ->
7       dService.list().then { dragons ->
8         render(toJson(dragons))
9       }
10    }
11  }
```

The system will automatically get the DragonService defined in the bindings when referenced as a parameter to a closure like dService.

Blocking

Blocking operations should be handled by using the blocking API. A blocking operation is anything that is IO-bound, such as querying the database.

The Blocking class is located at ratpack.exec.Blocking. For example, the following handler calls a method on the database (which is defined outside of the scope of this example):

```
1   get("deleteOlderThan/:days") {
2     int days = pathTokens.days as int
3     Blocking.get { database.deleteOlderThan(days) }
4             .then { int i -> render("$i records deleted") }
5   }
```

You can chain multiple blocking calls using the then method. The result of the previous closure is passed as the parameter to the next closure (an int in the preceding handler).

🔍 **Tip**   Blocking.get returns a ratpack.exec.Promise<T>.

Ratpack handles the thread scheduling for you and then joins with the original computation thread. This way, you can rejoin with the original HTTP request thread and return a result.

```
1   get("deleteOlderThan/:days") {
2     int days = pathTokens.days as int
3     int result
4     Blocking.get { database.deleteOlderThan(days) }
5             .then { int count -> result = count }
6     render("$result records deleted")
7   }
```

If no return value is required, use the Blocking.exec method.

Configuration

Any self-respecting web application should allow configuration to come from multiple locations: the application, the filesystem, environment variables, and system properties. This is a good practice in general, but especially for cloud-native apps.

Ratpack includes a built-in configuration API. The interface `ratpack.config.ConfigData` and its methods allow you to layer multiple sources of configuration. Using the `of` method with a passed closure allows you to define a factory of sorts for configuration from JSON, YAML, and other sources.

First, you define your configuration classes. These classes' properties will define the names of your configuration properties. For example:

```
1  class Config {
2        DatabaseConfig database
3  }
4  class DatabaseConfig {
5        String username = "root"
6        String password = ""
7        String hostname = "localhost"
8        String database = "myDb"
9  }
```

In this case, your JSON configuration might look like the following:

```
1  {
2        "database": {
3              "username":  "user",
4              "password":  "changeme",
5              "hostname":  "myapp.dev.company.com"
6        }
7  }
```

Later, in the `binding` declaration, add the following to bind the configuration defined by the previous classes:

```
1   def configData = ConfigData.of { d -> d.
2       json(getResource("/config.json")).
3       yaml(getResource("/config.yml")).
4       sysProps().
5       env().build()
6   }
7   bindInstance(configData.get(Config))
```

Each declaration overrides the previous declarations. So in this case, the order would be class definition, `config.json`, `config.yml`, system properties, and then environment variables. This way you could override properties at runtime.

System property and environment variable configuration must be prefixed with the `ratpack.` and `RATPACK_` prefixes. For example, the `hostname` property would be `ratpack.database.hostname` as a system property or `RATPACK_DATABASE_HOSTNAME` as environment variable.

Testing

Ratpack includes many test fixtures for aiding your unit, functional, and integration tests. It assumes you'll be using Spock to test your application.

First, if you're using the Ratpack-Gradle plugin, simply add the following dependencies:

```
1   dependencies {
2       testCompile ratpack.dependency('test')
3       testCompile "org.spockframework:spock-core:1.3-groovy-2.5"
4       testCompile 'cglib:cglib:3.2.12'
5       testCompile 'org.objenesis:objenesis:3.0.1'
6   }
```

The cglib and objenesis dependencies are needed for class and final class mocking.

Second, add your Spock tests under the src/test/groovy directory using the same package structure as your main project. A simple test might look like the following:

```
1    package myapp.services
2    import spock.lang.Specification
3
4    class MyServiceSpec extends Specification {
5        void "default service should return Hello World"() {
6            setup:
7            "Set up the service for testing"
8            def service = new  MyService()
9            when:
10             "Perform the service call"
11             def result = service.doStuff()
12             then:
13             "Ensure that the service call returned the proper
                result"
14             result == "Hello World"
15             "Shutdown the service when this feature is
                complete"
16             service.shutdown()
17        }
18   }
```

Ratpack enables your functional tests by running your full application within a test environment using GroovyRatpackMainApplicationUnderTest. For example, the following test would test the text rendered by your default handler:

```
1   package myapp
2   import    ratpack.groovy.test.GroovyRatpackMainApplication
              UnderTest
3   import spock.lang.Specification
4
5   class FunctionalSpec extends Specification {
6       void "default handler should render Hello World"() {
7           setup:
8           def aut = new GroovyRatpackMainApplicationUnderTest()
9           when:
10           def response = aut.httpClient.text
11          then:
12          response == "Hello World!"
13          cleanup:
14          aut.close()
15      }
16  }
```

Merely calling text on the httpClient invokes a GET request. However, more complex requests can be invoked using requestSpec. For example, to test a specific response is returned based on the User-Agent header:

```
1   void "should properly render for v2.0 clients"() {
2       when:
3       def response = aut.httpClient.requestSpec { spec ->
4           spec.headers.'User-Agent' = ["Client v2.0"]
5       }.get("api").body.text
6       then:
7       response == "V2 Model"
8   }
```

Summary

This chapter taught you about the following:

- How to get started with Ratpack

- Using handlers

- How to use bindings as a plugin architecture and for decoupling your modules

- How to render using Groovy Markup, Groovy Text, Thymeleaf, and Handlebars templates

- How to render and parse JSON

- Doing blocking operations

- Configuring a Ratpack app

- Testing a Ratpack app

ℹ Info   For more information, check out the Ratpack API.[4] Also consider *Learning Ratpack*[5] by Dan Woods.

---

[4]https://ratpack.io/manual/1.6.1/api/index.html
[5]http://shop.oreilly.com/product/0636920037545.do

Index

A

Abstract Syntax Tree (AST)
        transformations, 44
after method, 128
afterView method, 128
assets directory, 112
@AutoFinal, 22
@AutoImplement, 22

B

before method, 128
Boolean-resolution/Groovy
        truth, 49
breathFire method, 88
Build framework, 101
Build/images directory, 112

C

Closures, 12, 13
Cloud computing frameworks
    Caelyf, 101
    GAE, 100
@CompileStatic
        annotation, 16
ConfigSlurper, 38
Curry method, 87, 88

D

@Delegate annotation, 58
@DelegatesTo(SMS) annotation, 63
Delegation, 58
Dependency injection (DI), 137
deploymentPassword
        variables, 110
Design patterns
    delegation, 58
    metaClass method, 58
    meta-programming
        category, 55, 56
        meta-class, 55
    missing methods, 57
Domain-specific languages (DSLs)
    closure delegate, 61–63
    command chains, 63, 64
    extension modules, 70, 71
    methodMissing method, 67, 69
    override operators, 64–66
    propertyMissing method, 70
Dragon class, 95

E

eatDonuts() method, 59
Elvis operator, 17
Expando class, 39

© Adam L. Davis 2019
A. L. Davis, *Learning Groovy 3*, https://doi.org/10.1007/978-1-4842-5058-7